IAN PROCTOR . 1948

To Peter
from Mum & Dad.

11th Sept. 1954.

RACING DINGHY
MAINTENANCE

The bottom of one of the most famous of *National 12-footers* being polished by her skipper before a race at Bourne End, on the River Thames.

RACING DINGHY MAINTENANCE

by

IAN PROCTOR

SOUTHAMPTON
ROBERT ROSS & CO. LTD.
IN ASSOCIATION WITH
GEORGE G. HARRAP & CO. LTD.
LONDON   SIDNEY   TORONTO

To my mother and father

who were responsible for the maintenance

of myself for many seasons

First Published January, 1949
Second Edition July, 1951

PRINTED IN GREAT BRITAIN
BY W. & J. MACKAY & CO., LTD., CHATHAM, ENGLAND

PREFACE

THE proper maintenance of a racing dinghy is not difficult nor is it expensive, but it may justifiably be called an art. Moreover it is an art which is rapidly becoming specialised and, as such, demands a certain amount of study if it is to be practised successfully. Whether or not an owner has the time or the facilities to carry out his own maintenance work, a sound knowledge of what is involved is frequently required of him if he is to be able to direct the boatyard doing the work so that they may carry it out to his satisfaction, for many boatyards have little practical experience of the type of craft under consideration.

Racing dinghies are often sailed brutally hard in heavy weather, nearer to the limit of the strength of their gear than any other type of sailing boat is normally expected to venture. Similarly, in light weather, much is expected of them and, to be successful, the almost frictionless hulls must slide along under the influence of practically no wind at all. Such demands upon a boat under such varying conditions require her to be maintained with skill and understanding.

Designers may cudgel their brains, boat-builders put forth their greatest skill, sailmakers give of their best, helmsman and crew demonstrate their mastery of tactics and handling, but all this effort will be entirely wasted and the chance of winning a race thrown away if a tiny, but vital, piece of wire breaks because negligence has allowed it to rust and the mast goes over the side of the boat. The correct maintenance of a racing dinghy is of no less importance as a race-winning factor than is her proper handling or a full understanding of the rules under which she is raced.

Great ability on the part of a helmsman may win races against less skilful competitors even though he be sailing a poorly kept and ill-tuned boat, but he will meet with no success against equally expert helmsmen in dinghies kept at concert pitch. No racing dinghy helmsman, whatever his ability, can afford to be so complacent and satisfied with his skill as to neglect his boat.

An owner may allow himself to be consoled by the kindly comment of " bad luck " from a friend because he loses a race on account of failure in his boat's gear, but he should not allow himself to be deceived by it. In ninety-nine cases out of a hundred, broken gear is not bad luck but bad maintenance.

The attractions of dinghy sailing are many and varied. There is

5

the enjoyment of being afloat and getting healthy exercise in the open air ; the satisfaction of having secured a tactical victory and outsailed one's competitors is another source of delight, while the appreciation of the skill of someone else in sailing a better race should not fail to arouse pleasure and interest. By no means least amongst the joys of racing dinghies is the thrill of ownership of a boat in perfect condition, which reflects not only skill and patient care, but good sense and sound seamanship.

It is hoped, therefore, that not only will this book be a source of interest and knowledge, but also, indirectly, a source of pleasure, a spur to successful racing and a guide to proud ownership.

I wish to express my appreciation of the help which Gilbert Adams has rendered to me by allowing me to choose all the photographs for this work, except that on page 37, from his fine collection. My thanks are also due to Jimmy Ledwith, of Cellon, Ltd., who gave me valuable information for Chapter IV.

September, 1948.   IAN PROCTOR

NOTE ON THE SECOND EDITION

THE first edition of this book having been exhausted fairly rapidly, it has not been necessary to make many alterations in the second edition. However, some alterations and additions have been made which I hope will bring it up to date with recent advances and the use of new materials.

There are, in Great Britain alone, many thousands of racing dinghies and the number of hours of maintenance work expended upon them must be considerable. The collective experience of all those who read this book is immense compared with my own personal experience. As a simple example, if I varnish a dinghy with a certain brand of varnish it may take me two or three years to find out if that one brand stands up properly to use on a racing dinghy ; a dozen other people can be testing a dozen other brands in the meantime. I am therefore always grateful to hear from people who have found better ways of doing things than I use, or have discovered better materials.

July, 1951.   IAN PROCTOR

CONTENTS

RACING DINGHY MAINTENANCE

CHAPTER I

PERIODIC SURVEY AND FIRST AID

When to refit—Checking gear—First aid

I T was originally intended to head this chapter "Seasonal Survey." However, though the word "season" has its applications to most other forms of yachting and, indeed, to almost all sports, it is losing much of its significance in the dinghy world in Great Britain. At some racing centres, no sooner has the summer season ended than the winter season commences. On the river Thames, club fleets of as many as forty in a race are not exceptional in mid-winter and there are a number of important open races for a variety of classes held during the time of year which a few years ago was considered by most to be the close season. For the really enthusiastic dinghy helmsman, summer racing offers few more attractions than winter racing, so long as the right competition is always available. Indeed, on many stretches of inland water, I should say that the sailing is better by far when the trees are somewhat denuded of their blankety-blank blanketing leaves !

Since the main difference between the summer and winter season in these days would frequently seem to be only in the amount of clothes worn, " season " is obviously an obsolete term for many.

Under such conditions it may not always be easy to decide when best to carry out the maintenance work which every crack racing dinghy demands, if she is to have a chance of being kept at the head of the fleet for a number of years.

Whether a dinghy is raced throughout the year or only in the summer, her owner should plan his maintenance schedule according to her racing programme. Fixture cards for summer events are usually published early in the new year and the larger and more important winter events are generally on approximately the same dates year after year. It is therefore possible to plan, to a large extent, the year's sailing activities well in advance. It will then be easy to select the most suitable time for maintenance work.

Those who object to sailing with their feet in the half-frozen slush of spray water in the bottom of the dinghy, will obviously select the winter for their main refitting operations and, if they are wise, will commence the task as soon as they decide to sail no longer.

The hardy perpetuals have a less obvious choice. Furthermore they will probably have to do a fair amount of maintenance work at two periods during the racing year. Every dinghy sailor will have his own ideas on this subject—if he has any ideas at all and does not just leave his boat until she is in painful need of attention. My own preference is for doing the job in midwinter and midsummer.

The reasons for the choice of these times are several. In the first place, midwinter is, as a rule, comparatively free of the more important Open Races for Frostbiters, which mostly occur in the autumn and the spring ; there also generally seems to be a hiatus in the summer season, somewhere near the middle. Secondly, the wind in midsummer and midwinter *tends* to be lighter than at other times and therefore hull finish and high-pitch tuning is likely to be of more importance. Thirdly, as most of the important races for many dinghy classes are held towards the end of the summer season, the boat will be in the pink of condition at that time—not just freshly refitted, but also settled down again and back at concert-pitch. New rigging will have had time to stretch and splices to bed down before the more important events are sailed and before the heaviest weather may normally be expected. Fourthly, such a programme allows the winter work to be done when sailing will be least missed (those cold, clammy, foggy and windless December days) and the summer work to be done when a rest from racing can be most beneficial to a helmsman in preventing staleness and lack of tactical originality. It is hard to forego a sparkling summer week-end afloat and spend it cooped up in a stuffy boathouse while you struggle with sandpaper, varnish and wire rope, but such sacrifices are usually generously rewarded. As I have said, these are my own personal views and the reasons for them. Others may have equally good reasons for doing the job at some other time of the year.

In the case of the all-the-year-round enthusiast, one of his dinghy's refits will be most thorough and will generally be that which is done in the winter. The summer refit will then be nothing much more than a general sprucing-up of the boat's hull and a thorough check of all her gear and rigging.

As far as the finish of the hull is concerned, it should in the summer merely be necessary to rub down the surface of the outside with very fine sandpaper, steel wool or pumice powder to produce a good keying surface for a thin coat of finishing material. Any scars or bare patches should have been varnished or painted as soon as they were noticed, before the weather was able to discolour the wood ; these places should be touched up a little, so that the timber is given adequate protection before the finishing coat is applied. Gunwales and side decks, which come in for a lot of heavy wear, and the mast where the foresheets chafe against it, should also be reinforced by a thin coat of whatever protective is being used. Apart from this light coat, no more need be done and the more thorough cutting down of the surface and the application of a somewhat heavier coat of finish may be left to the winter.

The preparation of the hull and the application of the winter coat of finish is the same as is suggested for the treatment of the hull immediately before and during the application of the final coat of varnish or enamel to a newly built-up surface and is described in Chapters VI and VII on varnishing and enamelling.

The winter refit is the more important and is really the same whether the dinghy is being raced throughout the year or only in the summer. Most of the tasks which will be undertaken at this time are dealt with in the following chapters, in which will be set forth the majority of jobs which are likely to concern the dinghy owner. There is therefore no need to deal in detail with these jobs here, except that it should perhaps be emphasised that most standing and running rigging should generally be renewed as a matter of course.

The wise dinghy owner will check his craft's gear very frequently to make certain that everything is in proper order. A number of helmsmen choose to do this before every race and I do not believe that this is too often, but it is suggested that *after* every race is a better time to do it. Of course there is a very strong temptation to pack the boat away in the shortest possible time when a race is over, to clamber into glad-rags and to dash off to lend body to the clapping and general celebrations which honour the victor ; and it is right and proper that all competitors should make an effort to be present at the giving of the prizes. If, however, an opportunity presents itself in which it is possible to check over the dinghy's gear after the race and before dark, how much better is this than to leave it until before the next race, when anyway it will very possibly be too late to do anything about faulty or weakened gear, with the result that its discovery may cause anxiety throughout the race. The ideal to aim at is a check of your gear after a race, before you leave your boat for the night ; you will then have the chance to replace anything which is not quite up to scratch in plenty of time before your next sail.

Any gear which is continually needing repair should be noted and the cause sought. It may then be possible to remove the source of the trouble, by altering the lead of running gear or affording protection from chafe, when next a refit is being carried out.

The keeping of a rough log book for your dinghy is a practice which is very well worth while. In it can be entered her racing record and notes of how she performs under different conditions of wind and sea, with various mast rakes and dispositions of the weight of the crew and so on. In this way you will be able to make an extremely interesting study of what you are able to get out of your boat under conditions which you may know are not the most suitable for her. It is only in this way that the peak of tune can be attained and maintained. For those who are fortunate enough to be able to race very frequently, such notes should not really be necessary—though even for them they will be found helpful—but for those who are only seldom able to spare the time to race their boats, a log book of this nature is almost an essential, if a good performance is to be expected.

Intelligent study of the behaviour and reactions of one racing dinghy will lead to the rapid analysis and understanding of boats which are strange to the helmsman. The real expert can get into any dinghy—even of a class strange to him—and very soon get the best out of her. It is hard to say exactly how he may be able to accomplish this, but the main secret lies in the rapid analysis of the traits in her character, which he is quick to observe and treat with diplomatic understanding. Such a study will bring the knowledge of where to look for trouble in the boat's gear and will assist in her correct maintenance. Experience will enable the careful owner to carry out his surveys very quickly and thoroughly.

A good boat cover is essential if a dinghy is to be kept out of doors and maintenance work reduced to a minimum. A great weight of rain water in a dinghy is very bad for her shape and will strain the hull, quite apart from the fact that the planking will absorb some of the water and the weight of the boat may be much increased thereby. Excellent reproofing liquids may be had and are generally very easy to apply properly. But even the best of boat covers, most carefully proofed, will soon be pulled out of shape and deteriorate if large puddles of water are allowed to accumulate on it.

Many devices have been used to try and drain the water off boat covers. Some of them are rigged like tents, with ridge poles from the gooseneck to the transom, so that the cover forms a roof and the water runs over the sides. Other covers are put on over curved battens extending from gunwale to gunwale. None of these methods is really satisfactory ; they are very hard to put on and eventually puddles begin to form, the weight of the water in these increasing the hollows so that the trouble is accelerated. The answer to the problem is to cease the struggle against hollows and pools in the cover, because they are bound to occur in time in spite of all precautions. Figure 1 shows a cover which is efficient because the pools of water are not permitted to collect. It is a simple boat cover in which a canvas pipe is sewn into the natural hollow formed in it. The pipe is tucked into the centreboard case and drains off all the water from the cover.

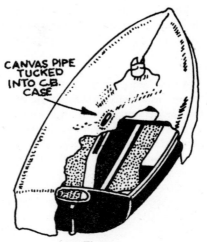

Figure 1

"A stitch in time saves nine" is an old proverb which applies very aptly to dinghy maintenance. A dab of varnish on a new scar, where the bare wood has been exposed, may save an hour's work when the time comes to refit. A few minutes with a sewing machine may stop a weakened seam in a sail from ripping adrift and necessitating expensive attention from a sailmaker later on. A little first-aid may be able to save a deal of time and patience.

When revarnishing (or re-enamelling) a dinghy at the periodic refit, the principles to be followed will be found in Chapter VI, the hull being treated as in the case of the last coat—though it may sometimes be thinner. If the boat is sailed on water where there are many powered marine craft in use, there may be a greasy deposit on the surface of the hull. It may not at first be apparent but will quickly clog ordinary dry sandpaper and it should be washed off with soap and water or wiped off with a turpentiney rag before rubbing down commences. If waterproof sandpaper is being used wet with a little soap, as recommended in Chapter VI, page 75, it will not be necessary first to wash the hull down.

Most dinghy owners wash the salt off their hulls after sailing on the sea. Many are of the opinion that salt water has a more detrimental effect on varnish and enamel than has fresh ; this is not so and the mineral salts in solution in many of our lakes and rivers will have a far more serious effect on the modern finishes immersed in them than will sea water. The object behind the washing off of the salt should be to remove the crystals which form a hard crust on the planking and which, apart from being almost continuously damp, may also remain in a crystallised form for some time before dissolving when the boat is once more afloat and may therefore cause added skin friction.

Fittings, cordage and sails should also be rinsed free of salt when the boat is brought ashore from a sail on salt water. This is dealt with more fully in later chapters on the various items mentioned.

* * * * *

A dinghy frequently gets scratched or bumped during her racing career, especially if she has to be stored in a boathouse or man-handled ashore more than is usual. As a rule such scratches do not go down to the bare wood, in which case there is no need to bother about them, but sometimes they are deep and the wood is exposed or even torn to a certain extent, as in Figure 2, which shows a much magnified section through the wood and varnish or enamel. In this case the place should be rubbed down slightly and any frayed ends of wood cut off with a knife, chisel or razor blade ; see Figure 3. A stopping material of some sort, such as the special coloured stopper made by some of the leading enamel and varnish manufacturers, should then be knifed well into the depression. It can then be smoothed off with a thin-bladed knife, such as an artist's palette knife, which has been dipped in turpentine.

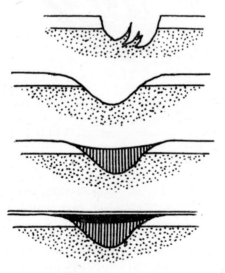

Figures 2, 3, 4 and 5

Any remaining surplus around the edges can be cleaned off with a rag moistened with turpentine, which should also be lightly passed across the filler in the scar itself. This will have the effect of bringing the level of the filler in the scar just below that of the surrounding varnish, as in Figure 4, and will allow sufficient depth for a few coats of varnish eventually to level off the surface uniformly. The patch should then be touched up or brought forward with a little varnish or enamel.

The terms " touching-up " and " bringing-forward "—the latter being that used by house decorators—are more or less self-explanatory. The object is to bring the level of the depression up to that of the general surface. The best thing with which to do this is a finger-tip dipped in the varnish or enamel. It is a messy job, but it is done better this way than with a brush, for it is easier to taper off the finish towards the edges and so prevent a ridge being formed around the patch. A fine-haired brush can sometimes be used, but it will generally be found more difficult. Figure 5 shows how the varnish is tapered off level with that surrounding it and how the overall finishing coat, applied at the periodic refit, will leave a perfectly smooth surface.

If a deep scratch should occur shortly before the boat is put afloat and there is no time to carry out the first-aid mentioned, a dab of varnish or some protective finish should be applied to the bare wood immediately. Even if this gets wet before it has time to harden, it will prevent water from getting to the wood, thereby preventing it from becoming saturated or discoloured.

Sometimes a single-skinned boat will open up if she has been out of the water for a long time or has been trailed in hot sunny weather, and she may leak considerably when she is launched. This is most likely to happen to carvel boats, but clinker-built dinghies do also leak occasionally. Very often the leaking will occur along the bottom of the centreboard case. The reason for this is that frequently the inside of the centreboard case is inadequately covered with paint and so rapidly absorbs or loses moisture on being immersed or dried out. The swelling and shrinkage of the timber which this causes is liable to be the source of leakage and is aggravated by the strains which trailing may impose on this part of the dinghy if she is being hauled behind a car for any great distance.

A little varnish applied in the angle between the centreboard case and the keelson inside the dinghy will usually cure this trouble immediately. If the boat is not to be used for a day or two, a little water poured into the bottom will soak into the wood sufficiently to cause it to swell and stop the gap. Only a *little* water is required to do this. I once witnessed the ghastly sight of a racing dinghy—the property of a large yacht club—which had been filled to capacity by the club boatman with a hose which was still pouring in water as fast as it spurted out from leaky seams and overflowed through the centreboard case. The pressure of the water was causing some of the planks to spring away from the stem on one side. I shudder to think how many hundredweights of water there were in that boat.

If the leakage in a carvel boat is too bad for her to take up by water being put into her, or by her being sailed around with a pump aboard for the first day or so, the offending seams should not be filled with some incompressible material, such as caulking cotton or putty, which will in time become hard. (This, of course applies only to small boats, the planks of which butt directly against one another and which rely on a good fit between the plank edges for their water-tightness. Larger hulls are normally caulked.) The effect of stopping the gap with a relatively incompressible material would be to strain the fastenings as the wood swelled back to its normal position and, also, to cause greater leaks later in the life of the boat. It is also a mistake to brush paint into the cracks between shrunken planks a long time before a dinghy is to be put afloat, as the paint will harden and forcibly prevent the planks from coming together as they swell. Recently applied finishes will not be hard enough to do this and will be squeezed out along the line of the seams as the planks swell. It is frequently necessary to scrape or cut off this exuded material when the boat has taken up.

As has been mentioned previously, seams which are too widely opened to make the flotation of the boat practical can be closed by letting the planks soak up moisture before the boat is put afloat. Unless a hose can be left slowly discharging water into the hull at the same rate as it runs out through the leaking seams, there is no very simple way of doing this. It is not generally possible properly to control the amount of water running into a boat in this way, and unless it is watched all the time, there is a danger of too much water accumulating as the planks take up and the gaps in the seams are reduced, so that, eventually, the hull will be filled with water and strained in consequence. A safer way of doing the job is to turn the hull upside down and spread wet sacks over it for a day or two. A whole day will frequently be sufficient to allow quite large cracks to fill in. Another method which is quite good if only one or two seams are leaking and it is desired to use the boat right away, is to stick strips of adhesive tape along the offending cracks. When the hull has become tight, the tape may be removed and any of the sticky material wiped off with a cloth and a little methylated spirit. Other suitable adhesive strip material, besides surgical plaster, is made and the now common transparent plastic film with a transparent adhesive is quite suitable and is almost invisible when stuck to the hull. An elastic stopper may also be used and, if pressed *over* the seam rather than *into* it, it may easily be scraped off later and cleaned up with a rag moistened in turpentine or paraffin.

It is always as well to carry a roll of some sort of adhesive strip for dealing temporarily with planks which may be cracked while racing or by an accident when the boat is being transported or lifted. Adhesive tape also comes in handy for a variety of different jobs, not only concerning the hull, but also the rigging and the crew !

As in the case of a leaky seam, no attempt should be made to cure leakage through a split plank by stuffing caulking cotton into the crack. This will merely aggravate the situation and is very likely to make the split run further. An attempt should be made to draw together the wood on either side of the crack and hold it there. This is usually done by permanently fastening a tingle strake to the inside of the hull, or simply by through fastening the plank on either side of the crack to the adjacent timbers. Figure 6 shows how a tingle strake is applied and no further explanation is needed : a little paint should be worked into the crack from the inside and be applied to the underside of the tingle before it is fastened.

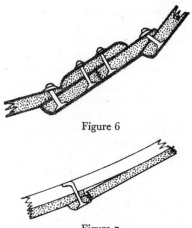

Figure 6

Unfortunately, in clinker-built boats, planks are apt to crack at the edge of the land or overlap, as shown in Figure 7. If this is the case, an ordinary tingle strake cannot be of much service and the best method of securing it is to fit a wedge-shaped piece of wood in

Figure 7

the gap between the rib and the inside of the upper plank. The cracked plank can then be fastened through the wedge and the rib with nails clenched over or riveted over rooves. (See Chapter IX, page 86.) Figure 8 shows the job completed. If, before the wedges are fitted and fastened, a little synthetic resin glue can be worked into the crack, this will make a very good job of it, for it will both seal it and make it tight ; if glue cannot be used, some paint or varnish should be brushed into the crack before fastening.

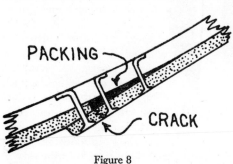

PACKING

CRACK

Figure 8

The extreme misfortune of having a plank or two stove-in while racing is rather beyond the scope of this book. As a very rough first-aid measure, however, a tingle strake can usually be fastened to the outside of the planking ; since such damage generally only occurs well above the waterline, such a repair might enable a dinghy competing in a series of races to complete the series without suffering much disadvantage, instead of having to abandon the contest. Not much ingenuity is needed when applying a tingle of this nature. Sometimes a sort of gasket (the word is used in its engineering, rather than nautical, sense) may be made to surround the hole and the tingle fastened over this to make a thoroughly water-tight job. The idea of tacking a messy patch on to the sleek hull of his boat may be upsetting to the dinghy-owner, but he should remember that, in all probability, the eventual repair will necessi-tate the removal of the damaged planks for some distance on either side of the wound and he should choose the positions for the fasten-ings of the patch so that they are made through planks and timbers which will, in any case, have to be removed and replaced later on. Every racing dinghy helmsman should carry a few pieces of water-proof plywood in his tool kit, so that he may have available the material for such a patch.

A more frequent and far less serious piece of damage is the chipping of a small sliver of wood from the leading edge of an unbound or unprotected rudder blade. Sometimes the piece nicked out will only

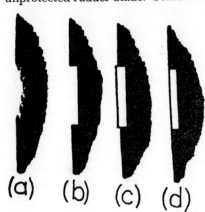

be very small and a match-stick can be used for the repair. Figure 9 shows how this simple repair is carried out. The first stage is to trim up the jagged edges around the nick and square off the ends. A match-stick, or other piece of wood, is then cut to the right length. A synthetic resinous glue is then applied to this and to the edges of the cleaned-up nick, whereupon the filling piece is stuck in position. If a

(a) (b) (c) (d)

Figure 9

gap-filling type of glue is used, there should be no difficulty in making good joints, even if the only tool used is a penknife. The glue is allowed to harden and the filling piece is then trimmed down to the right shape and taper with a knife, chisel or razor blade, finally being varnished or enamelled. Such little jobs of inlay work may seem somewhat crude, but they are effective and can be done in

18

Launching a *Firefly* at Henley. More damage is done to the hull of a dinghy during launching and hauling out than at any other time. With plenty of hands to help and a good soft mat to pad the concrete steps, this boat should be safe enough.

a few minutes' working time. They prevent nasty little eddies twisting over the surface of the rudder blade and so increasing its drag and reducing its efficiency.

There are a host of other first-aid jobs too numerous to mention here. Many of them will be touched upon in later and more specialised chapters.

CHAPTER II

RIGGING—WIRE AND WIRE ROPE

Standing rigging—Types of wire rope—Swaged end fittings—Splicing wire rope—Flexible wire rope—Piano wire

THE care of the rigging of a racing dinghy is probably the most important of all the maintenance tasks. It is a question of all or nothing. Your mast either stands or falls according to the state of your shrouds and stays. A badly maintained hull finish may mean a poorly performing boat, but a badly maintained set of rigging may mean that she is unable to perform at all and it may even be a source of danger.

If the hours or resources which can be spent on the upkeep of a dinghy are limited, it is better, by far, to spend what can be spared on the care of the rigging, rather than on the fussing about with her bottom finish.

Rigging is generally divided into two categories—standing rigging and running rigging. Standing rigging is, of course, that which is normally fixed so long as the boat is afloat and consists of shrouds, stays and so on. Running rigging is that which is used to move or trim sails, spars and other gear and consists of sheets, halliards, centreboard hoists, and so on.

However, for the purposes of consideration in this book, it is intended to divide the subject of rigging in a different manner. An attempt will be made to deal first with wire and wire rope rigging in this chapter and to devote the following chapter to cordage rigging.

Wire ropes are generally used on dinghies for shrouds, forestays and halliards and, in the bigger classes, they are also used for centreboard hoists and sometimes for reefing gear and kicking straps. It will be noted that they have a variety of duties to perform and it is not surprising that, to perform these widely differing tasks, ropes with greatly varying characteristics must be utilised.

The mainshrouds—the most important bits of rope in the vessel, except those which hold the skipper's trousers up—are generally of stranded steel wire rope of about three-eighth-inch circumference. To the average being that may seem clear enough, but to the rigger or wire rope specialist it means almost nothing, for there are about a couple of hundred different forms or constructions of wire ropes which are manufactured for widely differing purposes and have widely differing characteristics. The rope may also be made of a variety of materials, including several grades of mild steel, " best patent steel," " special improved patent," " best plough," " special improved plough " and stainless steels. Recently other alloys such as " Tungum," which is relatively light and highly resistant to corrosion, have been made up into wire ropes.

Dinghies' shrouds are commonly of best plough steel wire. Six single wires are twisted—generally in a left-hand direction—around a seventh to form a strand. Six strands are then twisted—in a right-hand direction—around a fibre core to form a rope. Such a construction is known as 6×7, i.e., six strands of seven wires each. The object of twisting the wires together in one direction and then twisting the strands so formed in the opposite direction, to make the rope, is so that the natural tendency of the wire to spring back to its original straight form, from the spiral into which it is twisted, is largely balanced.

Nearly everything to do with boats and their design is a compromise. In the case of shrouds, a rope with relatively large wires for its size is chosen, because this reduces the dangers of corrosion to each wire. A fibre core is used because, in spite of the fact that this increases stretch slightly, it also increases resistance to corrosion, for the fibre may be impregnated with an anti-corrosive substance which will help to retard the attacks of rust at the heart of the rope. Although a rope with good properties of flexibility is not particularly required, the slightly increased flexibility which the fibre core imparts is useful in rendering the rope more amenable to handling when making up and splicing into shrouds.

One cannot but wonder whether this type of rope is still the best for the particular job in question. We have considered its good points ; let us now look at its bad points. The main disadvantage is that its outer surface is very rough, as will be seen in Figure 10, and its wind resistance and disturbance of the airflow is therefore high. If corrosion can be reduced by increasing the diameter of the individual wires, why not increase them still further ? Stretch is a bad thing in standing rigging ; cannot we use a wire rope in which there is no stretch ? Granted the

Figure 10

fibre core makes splicing easier, but if splicing could be eliminated there would no longer be any need for the fibre core and the undesirable stretch which goes with it.

At first sight a single wire would seem to be the ideal and dinghies with such shrouds are not unknown. In certain cases at least (it would be unwise to be too dogmatic on the point) single wire main shrouds have not been a success. There is safety in numbers. One heavy blow on a single wire may bend and weaken it badly—and there is no other to help it in its task. Furthermore, there appears to be a tendency for the rapid vibrations which the wind may set up in solid rigging (causing the familiar humming), to produce crystallisation within the wire which may cause it to snap without warning. As has been said, these remarks are based on my own personal experiences and on observations of the experiences of others using the same material. The single wire shroud should not necessarily be condemned purely on such rather limited evidence, which to me, however, was sufficiently convincing to cause me to abandon its use after a very short time.

A so-called refinement of single wire rigging, which I feel should be condemned as unsuitable for dinghies, is the solid streamlined rod or bar rigging, which I believe originated in the U.S.A. This type of rigging is similar to that sometimes used on aircraft and is of a section which affords very little wind resistance when the air pressure is *directly ahead*. However, a sailing vessel is never in a position when the wind is directly ahead, except when she is in stays or wind-rode on moorings ! When she is sailing as close to the wind as possible, the apparent (effective) wind will be about 30 degrees off the bow, and at such an angle, rigging of streamlined section creates far more eddies than would an ordinary round - sectioned wire rope. Figure 11 will make this clear.

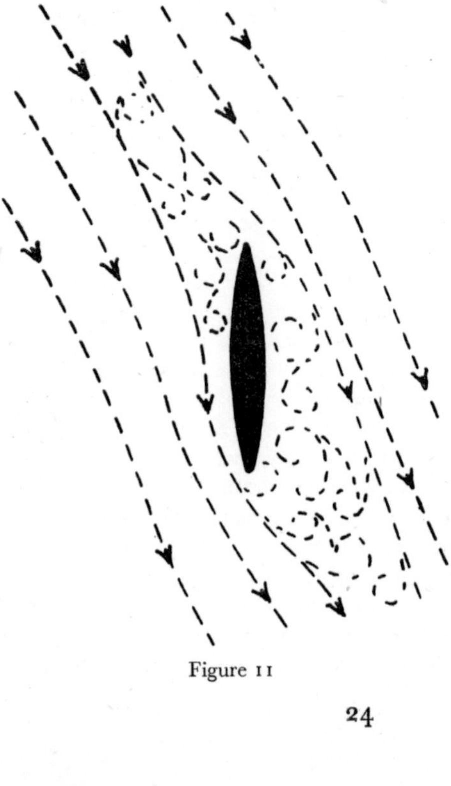

If, therefore, single wire or rod rigging is not considered suitable, what is the next best thing to give the minimum of resistance to the wind and the maximum of resistance to corrosion, at the same time being able to withstand hard knocks without being unduly weakened ? The answer is a rope made of 7, 19, or 27 single

Figure 11

24

wires, which will give a rope of fairly smooth section. Twenty-seven wires would seem to be the best and the appearance of this section is shown in Figure 12. It will be seen that the wind resistance of this type of rope will be relatively small when compared with that of the rope shown in Figure 10.

Let us now see what has to be sacrificed in other directions if such a rope of 27 single wires is used. In the first place it is less resistant to corrosion than is the single wire or, perhaps, the 6 × 7 construction with an anti-corrosive impregnated fibre core. Secondly, it is impossible to splice and not so easy to handle. In other respects it

Figure 12

is as satisfactory, or more so, than 6 × 7 or solid wire rigging. What can be done to mitigate the two disadvantages mentioned ? As far as the menace of corrosion is concerned, we can almost eliminate this by using stainless steel wire which can be rinsed in fresh water and periodically dressed with oil, when its life should be extreme. A new process of galvanising, known as Bryanising, in which the zinc is deposited electrically instead of by the old hot bath method, may also increase the resistance of ordinary steel rope to corrosion, for the thickness of the zinc coating may be accurately controlled and modified.

The second snag—the difficulty of splicing—can be overcome by not splicing at all, but swaging suitable end fittings (such as rigging screw ends and terminals with eyes or forks) on to the wire rope. This method of attaching terminal fittings has been used on aircraft for some time. The overall strength of a rope with swaged terminals is much greater than that with spliced ends, seeing that a reduction in the strength of the rope of 20 per cent is usually allowed for the splice. The attachment of swaged fittings is a task which cannot be undertaken without the suitable apparatus, which is simply a specially made press which squeezes the hollow end fitting into which the rope is inserted, thus forcing it tightly on to the rope which it grips firmly. Not only is such an end stronger, but it is also far neater and offers less resistance to the windstream. Furthermore, the stretch which is involved in a splice is eliminated ; the stretch in such a rope, with such fittings, is negligible. Incidentally, the work of swaging on end fittings can be done through certain boatyards which are agents for the wire rope manufacturers, who do the job themselves.

* * * * *

There are, however, many who will probably never take to rigging with swaged ends simply because they take a delight in doing their own rigging unaided ; it is not difficult to understand this point of view. The splicing of 6 × 7 wire rope for standing rigging is the same as for that used for running rigging, which is also generally made up of six strands. The features in the construction of wire rope for running rigging will be discussed a little later on and it is intended here merely to mention its construction of six strands, so that the method adopted in its splicing may be logically coupled with that used for the 6 × 7 rope for standing rigging. The method is as follows.

The rope is first measured off carefully and an allowance made for the stretch which will occur in new rope. One hundred feet of new wire rope of 6 × 7 construction will stretch $1\frac{1}{2}$ inches when loaded to one-tenth of its breaking load ; this will be about the strain which it will be expected to bear when in use as shrouds on a racing dinghy. If the load is doubled, the stretch will be $2\frac{1}{2}$ inches on the original hundred feet. This means to say that the stretch in a shroud of about sixteen feet (a length common to many racing dinghies), will be just under $\frac{1}{4}$-inch at one-tenth of the breaking load. The stretch of the splice and the bedding down of the eye on to the thimble will probably give another $\frac{1}{8}$-inch at each end, so that the total stretch over the completed shroud will be in the region of $\frac{1}{2}$-inch at normal working load. This must be allowed for and the new length should be such that the ends of the rigging screws are each entered into the body by about $\frac{3}{8}$-inch. This will then allow plenty of adjustment for the stretch to be taken up by a normal rigging screw.

The splice will nearly always be made around a thimble. The rope should be whipped or served at a sufficient distance from its end (about four or five inches in the case of dinghy shrouds), to allow enough length in the strands to permit them to be handled and tucked with ease. If it is desired to make a particularly neat job, the rope can be served over that part of it which is to lie around the perimeter of the thimble. Well-waxed seaming twine is suitable for making a neat serving on small wire ropes. The rope is then bent around the thimble and secured in place by temporary lashings. Figure 13 shows the operation at this stage. The whipping on the free end of the rope is then removed. Each strand must now be secured from unravelling without delay. This may be done by whipping them with thread, or by heating the tips of the strands and twisting the wires together with pliers whilst they are still hot. With some wire it may be found possible to secure the strands by tipping them with solder, which prevents unravelling.

The splice proper may now be made. There are at least six

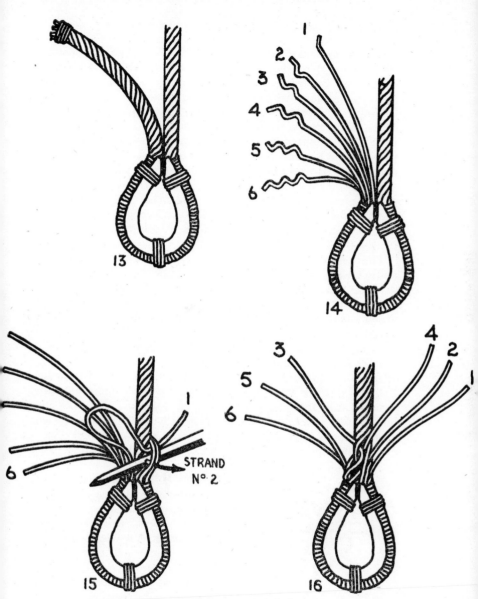

Figures 13, 14, 15 and 16

recognised ways of making a splice in six stranded wire rope, but the following is perhaps generally considered to be the most reliable.

The strands of the rope are opened out as in Figure 14, care being taken to keep them spread in an orderly fashion, so that there is no confusion over their arrangement. The fibre heart is cut out.

As an aid to identifying the various strands in the more advanced stages of the splice, it is a very sound idea to put a small bend in each strand according to the number of the strands ; thus strand No. 2 would have two bends in it, and strand No. 5, five bends in it, and so on (this is clearly shown in ·Figure 14, in which the size of the kinks is exaggerated for the sake of clarity). The marline spike is then inserted into the rope from right to left and lifting two strands, as in Figure 15 ; strand No. 1 is tucked away to the right— in the opposite direction to the insertion of the spike.

The spike is then withdrawn and inserted *between* the two strands which it raised for the first tuck to be made ; it therefore only raises the left hand of the two strands. Reference to Figure 15 will show where it is inserted. Strand No. 2 is tucked away to the right in a similar way to No. 1.

The next two tucks serve to lock the splice. The spike is inserted under the next strand to the left. Strand *No. 4* is then inserted over the spike and pulled away to the right, as in the two previous tucks. The spike is *not* withdrawn and strand No. 3 is inserted beneath the strand which is raised by the spike and tucked away in the same direction as that in which the spike was inserted, i.e., from right to left, or towards the point of the spike. Strands Nos. 3 and 4, therefore, go under the same strand of the standing part, but in opposite directions. Figure 16 shows how the splice should look at this stage.

The next strand to the left is then raised with the spike and No. 5 is tucked away behind and over the spike to the left. Strand No. 6 is tucked away in a similar manner under the next strand to the left. The first set of tucks is now complete and one strand should emerge from each depression between the strands of the standing part :

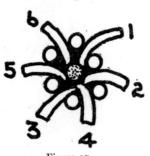

Figure 17

Figure 17 attempts to show this. The strands should be pulled and persuaded into positions in which they will lie fair. On no account should they be twisted or sharply bent during the tucking process. A few light taps with a mallet will be helpful in getting the strands to assume a good lie.

The second and succeeding series of tucks are very simple. Starting with No. 1, the strands are tucked away to the left, over one and under one of the strands in the standing part. The other five strands are tucked in a similar manner. Four sets of tucks are made in this way. Half the wires may then be cut from each strand and another tuck made to taper the splice. Alternatively, every other strand may be tucked once more in the usual way and cut off after the fifth tuck has been made, the remaining strands being cut off after the fourth tuck. Before the strands are cut off, the splice must be persuaded and cajoled (not cudgelled) into lying fair and even, so that the strands have the appearance of bedding down comfortably. A little light pummelling with a mallet will probably be helpful.

A liberal quantity of heavy grease should then be worked in around the splice. This will protect the wire, from which the marline spike may have scraped the protective zinc coat, from corrosion. Sometimes the splice is bound with tape at this stage, but if a neat and compact splice has been made, this should not be necessary. The splice is finally served with waxed twine securely bound around it. Generally a serving on a wire rope splice is commenced at the neck and works towards the thimble, but personally I prefer to start at the thimble and work towards the end of the splice ; in this manner it appears that the whole splice will lie more snugly and it is easier to catch in and hold down the springy ends of the wire where they are cut off. The most satisfactory knot with which to finish off a serving is a modified form of the flat knot, which is shown

Figure 18

in Figure 18. To make it neater and a little more secure, the free end may be tucked under the nearest strand of the wire rope.

* * * * *

The great majority of modern racing dinghies use wire rope halliards, for every effort is made to keep the luffs of the sails at a constant tautness and, of course, wire rope is much less susceptible to stretch or the effects of humidity than fibre cordage would be. Generally, dinghy halliards will be of 6 × 12 construction, with six wire strands laid up around a fibre core, each strand consisting of twelve single wires also laid up around a fibre core. The inclusion of the fibre cores in the strands and the relative fineness of the wires employed in the construction, are the elements which give flexibility to the rope, which is necessary if it is to render over sheaves smoothly and without damaging itself. Unfortunately, this essential feature of flexibility cannot be obtained without some sacrifice of resistance to stretch, for, when under load, the wires and strands will pull in on the fibre cores, compressing them slightly and thereby permitting elongation of the rope. However, satisfactory methods of taking up the stretch in halliards, whilst under way, can be provided in most racing dinghies.

The stretch in 100 feet of new 6 × 12 wire rope would be about 6½ inches at one tenth of the breaking load. This means that there may be as much as just over 2¼ inches' stretch in a foresail halliard on some *National 12-foot* dinghies, and rather more than one inch in the case of *International 14-footers ;* this does not include the stretch in the wire luff rope of the sail. It must be remembered, however, that some of this stretch will be permanent and so, after the rope has been under load several times, some of this initial stretch will remain. Nevertheless there will always be a certain amount of elasticity, which is the real bugbear of those who wish to keep the luffs of their foresails as straight as possible. The precise amount of stretch in most types of rope is impossible to give with any degree of accuracy, for where a vegetable fibre core is used there is a natural and variable factor ; it must therefore be realised that only a near approximation can be given.

Flexible wire rope is also used for the centreboard hoisting tackle on most dinghies using centreboard winches. This tackle has an exceedingly tough time and its expectation of life is not great. As the plate is raised one part of the wire will probably cross another, so that, on the drum or axle of the winch, the rope is badly nipped and crushed. Not only is this liable to cause the individual wires to break, but it will also scrape the protective zinc from the wire and leave it exposed to the corrosive attacks of rust. It is therefore most important to renew centreplate tackles frequently, especially if the plate is very heavy, for if the tackle should break, the plate might crash down and badly injure the crew or the boat. Of course, these remarks do not apply to dinghies with very light centreboards.

If a dinghy is stored for the winter and her rigging is sound and does not require renewal, every care should be taken to see that it does not deteriorate during the off-season. It should be rinsed in fresh water—preferably warm—to dissolve out any salt from the fibre cores. After drying, it should be dressed with oil or grease, or even left immersed in an oil bath. There are a number of personal faiths over the correct method of foiling the ravages of the rust menace. Some people advocate simply immersing the coiled wire ropes in thick oil until they are needed, but others claim that the constant immersion in oil has a tendency to soften the steel—though it seems unlikely that any such softening would be serious enough to do much harm. (Automobile engineers sometimes state that the spraying of car springs with oil has a tendency to soften them.) My own method is to dissolve some grease in petrol, or some other volatile solvent, and work this fluid mixture well into the rope, leaving a liberal quantity on the surface. The petrol thins the grease sufficiently to allow it to flow right into the heart of the rope and thoroughly impregnate the whole thing ; later, as the petrol evaporates, the thick and protecting grease is left where it can do most good. The surplus can be wiped off with a rag before the shrouds are put into use again. Rigging screws and shackles should receive similar attention.

In spite of every care being taken of the wire ropes on a racing dinghy, it is only seldom that they can really be trusted to give two years' service if the boat is being raced on salt water, unless the ropes are made of some non-corrosive material. It cannot be too strongly emphasised that no risks should be taken with them and, if there is the slightest reason for doubting their soundness, play for safety and replace them.

For the diamond shrouds (those which run over the spreaders or crosstrees) and the topmast stays of racing dinghies, solid high-tensile steel "piano" wire of about 17 gauge is generally used. Sometimes this wire is of stainless steel, but more usually it is galvanised.

The securing of the ends of piano wire around small thimbles is very simple. No allowance has to be made for stretch, which is negligible. First of all a small "stop" is made. I prefer to use a short length of copper or brass tubing for this job, slightly squeezing it to an oval cross-section so that the two lengths of the rigging wire will lie side by side in it as in Figure 19. However, small coils of steel wire are often used for the job and can be bought for the purpose. The stop is slipped on to the wire, which is then bent around the thimble and back alongside itself, as shown in Figure 19. The stop is then slipped up over the end of the wire and forced up as close as possible to the thimble, whereupon the end of the wire is bent back towards the thimble, thus keeping the stop in place. This is shown

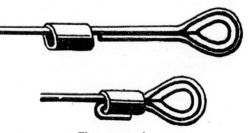

Figures 19 and 20

in Figure 20. Sometimes a small seizing is put on over the bent-back wire, and it is always advisable to cover the "splice" with adhesive tape to keep it from tearing holes in the sails. It is a good thing to cover the adhesive tape with varnish or dope to prevent water getting in, for the bends in the wire may cause the galvanising to crack and peel from it, thus rendering it susceptible to rust.

Kicking strap tackles made of wire will usually be of flexible stuff, but may also be of piano wire. In either case no special mention need be made about them here, for they will probably have a simple eye in both ends and the making of these has already been described in this chapter. They will usually have a tail made of hambro' line, or some other small stuff, which will be eyespliced to one of the eyes in the wire ; the making of an eyesplice in three-stranded cordage is described in the following chapter. Incidentally, the author favours kicking straps made of hambro' line entirely, having nearly beheaded one good crew with a piano wire affair and almost caused another to lose an ear on one made from wire rope !

A hambro'line kicking strap can, I believe, be set up sufficiently taut in the first place when the dinghy is on the wind to nullify the effects of stretch when strain comes on it when off the wind.

Apart from wire roller reefing tackle, which requires no special mention, this completes the list of wire and wire rope gear and we may now turn our attention to cordage.

* * *

High strain galvanised wire ropes covered by a thin layer of plastic have now been introduced into this country. This covering of plastic gives the wire rope a perfectly smooth finish, which helps to reduce wind resistance and completely seals it from corrosion. The plastic skin, though thin, is remarkably tough and even when cut can only be pulled from the wire with difficulty. Surprisingly, this rope is less than a third the cost of stainless steel wire and the breaking strains have been brought up to the equivalent of plough steel in the same circumferences without extra weight. Watertight splices can be made with the use of plastic tape and plastic sealing compound.

An additional covering of plastic tube may be used over portions of the shrouds liable to meet abrasion from foresail sheets and the smooth surface of the wire should eliminate the need for shroud rollers to reduce friction on sheets.

CHAPTER III

RIGGING—CORDAGE

Nylon rope—Eyes in plaited rope—Whipping—Foresail sheets—Tail splices—Eye splices

RECENTLY nylon ropes have been introduced into the sailing world and there is little doubt that they will prove to be a great benefit to dinghy sailors.

Though manilla and hemp give, respectively, hard and soft ropes of great strength and reliability, they are usually not smooth enough to render with the minimum of friction through blocks or fairleads. Furthermore they are inclined to be difficult to handle and to become stiff when wet. Dinghy owners therefore turned to cotton rope in the form of round sennit, plait or braid and this type of rope has been in general use in dinghies for a number of years. It has the advantage of being quite kink-proof, even when new ; nor does it stiffen when wet and it renders easily through blocks and fairleads. On the other hand it is very treacherous and susceptible to rot ; it is liable to break without warning, whilst its resistance to surface abrasion is poor and its retention of moisture is excessive.

Nylon is still rather a novelty ; though for some purposes it has advantages over cotton, it is more slippery to handle and is therefore more suitable in stranded rather than braided forms. It is soft and pliable under all conditions and is unaffected in any way by wet, except for an increase in weight of up to twenty per cent—mainly due to the retention of moisture between the fibres. Its tensile strength is very great and far in excess of that of manilla rope, whilst its elasticity (which is a disadvantage in cases where no stretch is desired, such as halliards in larger yachts) gives it an exceptional resistance to shock loads, which are the most common causes of failure in normal fibre ropes. Most people familiar with the sea know of the general use of coir or grassline ropes for towing ; these are used, not because they are stronger, but because they are more springy than hemp, manilla or sisal, and therefore are able to absorb the shocks which are liable to be put upon them when carrying out their particular task. Nylon is quite immune from rotting or decay and it stands up to surface abrasion better than does manilla and is far superior to cotton in this respect.

Were it not for the fact that cordage of a fairly large diameter has to be used for the sheets of dinghies—so that they may be handled with ease—nylon would provide a great saving in weight, for it is almost twice as strong as sisal rope and about forty-five per cent stronger than manilla under a steady load (much more than this under shock-load conditions). However, in spite of the fact that— for considerations other than strength—a smaller diameter rope than is normal cannot be used, a small saving in weight is made, for nylon rope is seventeen per cent lighter than manilla.

Nylon rope may be knotted, spliced, seized or served as cotton rope, except that, owing to the smoothness of its fibres, it is considered advisable to give five, rather than the normal three tucks when splicing. The following notes on the making up of sheets may therefore be taken to apply to both cotton and nylon material.

It is possible to form an eye in the end of round sennit or braided rope, of which dinghy sheets are usually made, in a number of different ways, some of which are rather complicated. The following method is simple and easy to accomplish and, if done skilfully, will hold well enough for its task.

Generally the mainsheet will be made fast direct to one of the mainsheet blocks, but occasionally an eye will be made around a thimble, which will be shackled to the block or other fitting. In either case the procedure is the same. A serving may be put on the rope from a distance of about three inches from its end ; the serving should be long enough to cover that part of the rope which is going to lie around the thimble or the eye of the block. If this is not done, a short whipping should be put on about three inches from the end

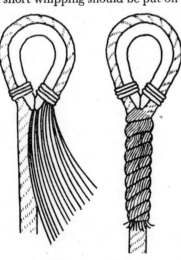

Figures 21 and 22

(see page 36 for details of a suitable whipping). The end of the rope is now unravelled into its component threads, which should be combed out flat with the fingers and thinned out towards their ends by scraping them with a knife against a flat board. The rope is then placed in position around the thimble or eye of the block and may be secured in position with a temporary lashing, if this is thought convenient. Figure 21 shows the eye at this stage. The threads are now wrapped spirally around the standing part of the rope, being

secured roughly in place with thread or light twine ; see Figure 22.
The neck is then tightly served with sailmaker's twine in the *same
direction* as that in which the threads are wrapped ; the thinning
of the threads towards their ends will cause the neck to taper down
smoothly. To make the eye more secure, the serving can be varnished
or, better still, given two or three applications of clear dope which
will shrink it up very tightly and make it waterproof.

Mainsheets may sometimes be used for two seasons if they are
turned end for end, so that the part which has to stand the heavy
strain when the dinghy is close-hauled is given a rest and only comes
into use when the boat is well off the wind and the strain is far less.
If you have any reason for doubting the soundness of your mainsheet,
renew it without hesitation, for it may well let you down when you
are most anxious for it not to. Nylon ropes should have a far greater
expectation of life, but even with a nylon mainsheet it may be
advisable to turn it end for end after every season, so that it gets a
rest and is evenly worn throughout.

Cotton sheets should always be rinsed out in fresh water periodically. They should then be made up into a large coil and allowed to
dry. Large coils allow plenty of air to get to the rope which will dry
more quickly. This will reduce the rot menace.

The ends of sheets are whipped to prevent them fraying. Owing
to the softness and compressibility of braided cordage, whippings
will stay on quite easily, if put on tightly, for they will constrict the
rope and bed down snugly, leaving a little topknot frayed out at the
end like the hairstyle of some native African lady. Almost any kind
of whipping will do and the common whipping is the simplest. However, the American whipping is rather better and will be explained
here.

To make an American whipping, one end of the whipping twine
is laid along the rope, pointing towards the rope's end. Several
turns are then taken around both the rope and the twine. When the
whipping is about as long as the diameter of the rope—or about half
as long again in the case of a nylon rope—a fairly large loop is formed
in the twine, the free end of which is laid back along the rope, away
from its end ; see Figure 23. About five or six more turns are taken,
with the twine in this loop, around both the rope and the twine
itself. The end is then pulled tight and the whipping will appear as
in Figure 24. The two ends of the twine may be tied with a reef knot
before cutting off.

Foresail sheets are generally secured to the clew of the sail with a
seizing, the two sheets being formed of a single length of rope, one
half of which acts as port sheet and the other half as starboard sheet.
The officially correct seizing to use for this job is what is known as

Figure 23   Figure 24

a round seizing. I have, however, found that a more simple flat seizing is quicker and easier to apply and always stands up to its task without any trouble. Figure 25 will show how this seizing is commenced by taking several turns with the twine around one of the standing parts of the sheet. This is done to a distance of about an inch and a half from the cleft of the eye.

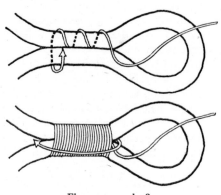

A number of round turns are then taken around both the standing parts and back to the cleft or straddle of the eye. The twine is then brought up through the eye by the cleft and passed down at the other end of the seizing, between the two standing parts of the rope. (See Figure 26.) Two or three crossing turns are made in this

Figures 25 and 26

manner over the round turns of the seizing and the two ends of the twine are knotted together with a reef knot at the cleft of the eye.

Sometimes the eye in foresail sheets is served over to prevent it wearing on the clew thimble of the sail, but since the sheet invariably first wears through at the portion which is in the fairlead when the dinghy is close-hauled, this is not an essential operation and the time which would be spent on it is better devoted to some other job.

Cotton foresail sheets should always be renewed every season, for their strength may be reduced by rot without it being apparent, so that no warning is given of its weakness. The abrasive action of deadeye fairleads on the rope will swiftly weaken it. Nylon rope

This photo shows that even successful boats, such as this *Merlin*, can often be improved by attention to small details. A little more flexibility at the inboard end of the sail battens would probably eliminate the ridge in the mainsail along the end of the batten pockets.

may be used until it shows signs of wear, for there is no danger of deterioration from other causes.

*　　*　　*　　*　　*

Quite frequently hambro' line or other small stuff tails are spliced into the ends of wire halliards. This is done so that the halliard may be cleated as short as possible, in order that there may be the least possible length of it to stretch. A wire rope halliard can only be cleated at its very end, for the act of bending it over the cleat puts permanent kinks in it, which both weaken it and may prevent it running through blocks or over sheaves. A rope tail can of course be cleated without any harm being done to it and, since there is so short a length of fibre rope actually under tension when the sail is set, the stretch in the two or three inches taking the strain is almost negligible. Figure 27 shows how a rope tail may be used.

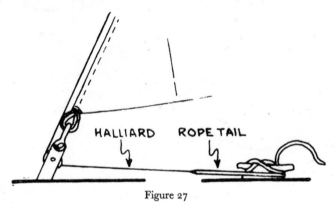

HALLIARD　　ROPE TAIL

Figure 27

The method of splicing a rope tail properly into a wire halliard with six strands is not difficult. The stuff used for the tail will generally be made up of three strands. The wire rope should there-fore be unstranded for about one and a half times the full length of the intended splice. The strands are then divided into pairs and bound together thus with tape or light seaming twine ; they are now laid up again for half their length. These paired strands of the wire rope and the three strands of the cordage tail are then short-spliced together in the normal way. Figure 28 shows the paired wire strands being intertwined with the strands of the rope tail ; this is the first stage of making the splice. It will be seen that the strands of one rope go alternately between the strands of the other. At this stage a temporary seizing may with advantage be put around the cordage strands embracing the wire rope.

c

The next stage in making the splice is to take one of the pairs of wire rope strands and to tuck it over one strand of the rope tail and under one strand ; the next pair in rotation is tucked in a similar manner (Figure 29) and finally the third pair follows. Each pair is

Figures 28 and 29

tucked three times altogether in this manner. If desired, the paired strands can then be untaped and one strand of each pair cut out, the remaining strand being tucked a fourth time. The temporary seizing, if applied, is now removed from the rope tail strands and these are then tucked over one paired strand of the wire rope and under one in exactly the same manner as that employed in the tucking of the strands of the wire rope into the strands of the cordage. Four tucks are taken in this way and the rope strands are then tapered by scraping them with a knife, after which a further two tucks are made to complete the splice. The whole splice is then served over with seaming twine.

The type of tail splice which is explained in the foregoing paragraphs is very strong and can be neat if well made, but it will be too bulky to pass through blocks. Generally rope tails will not be expected to pass through blocks which are also used for the wire rope of a halliard or other running gear, for it stands to reason that if the sheave of a block is suitable for the rope tail it can scarcely be suitable for the wire rope—and vice versa. A little ingenuity in the arrangement of the rigging can generally obviate the need for a block to serve two so widely differing sizes and textures of rope. However, if it is absolutely necessary for the splice of the rope tail to render through a block, there are tail splices which are rather less bulky than that given in this book. Nevertheless, they are sufficiently complicated to make their explanation take more space than can be spared here : the reader will be able to find the instructions for making such splices in *The Ashley Book of Knots* (Clifford W. Ashley—Faber, 52/6), which can probably be obtained from a good reference library.

The remaining rigging jobs concern only the splices and whippings put on such small stuff as is used for the tack outhauls or clew downhauls of mainsails and the parts of cordage kicking strap tackles.

It is generally best to secure the plain ends of small stranded stuff with a palm and needle whipping which is a more reliable and permanent way of securing a rope's end from fraying than is the common whipping put on without a needle or the American whipping which was described earlier in this chapter. As a matter of fact, this type of whipping can be done without the aid of a needle and palm—in spite of its name—though it is more easily done with the aid of these tools. The method employed is as follows : the needle is first inserted between two of the strands and almost the whole length of the twine is pulled through, only sufficient being left to form the final knot ; this is shown in Figure 30. A fair number of turns are then taken around the rope or cord—making the whipping about one and a half times as long as the diameter of the stuff to which it is being applied (less in the case of larger ropes). Each turn is pulled taut as it is applied. The end is then passed under one of the strands, as in

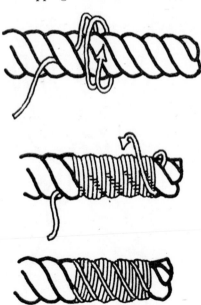

Figures 30, 31 and 32

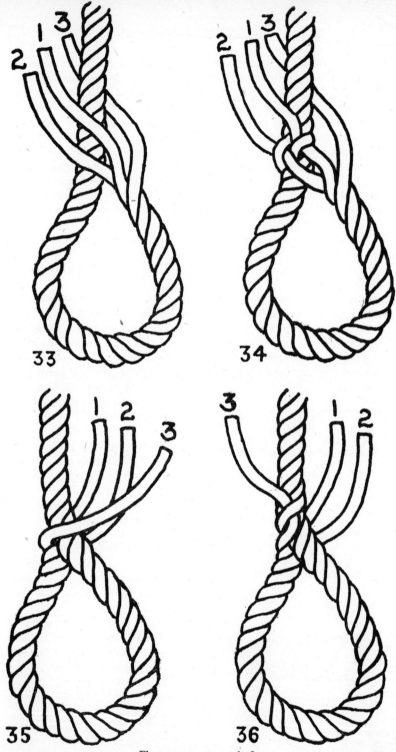

Figures 33, 34, 35 and 36

Figure 31, and then made to follow in the lay of the rope—between the two strands from between which it emerges—to the other end of the whipping, where it is again passed under a strand and brought back in the lay of the rope in the depression between the next two strands. It is then passed under the third strand and returned to the other end of the whipping in the third and only " unoccupied " depression. Finally it is passed under a strand and finished off neatly in a reef knot with the other end of the twine left loose for that purpose. The finished whipping is shown in Figure 32. The whipping is, of course, made neater and more secure if the twine is well beeswaxed before use.

Eye splices are generally put in the other end of most of the small items of cordage running gear, the eye being used to attach them to the thing which they control. An eye splice in three strand cordage is made thus : the rope is first unlaid into strands for a short distance from its end. The loop or eye is now formed in the end and the unlaid strands are arranged against the standing part as shown in Figure 33. The middle strand—No. 1—is then tucked against the lay of the rope under the most adjacent strand to it of the standing part. The next strand to the left, No. 2, is now passed over the strand of the standing part under which No. 1 is tucked, and is itself tucked under the strand next to this. Figure 34 shows this stage. The splice is next turned over and will then appear as in Figure 35. The remaining strand is now taken and tucked under the third strand of the standing part. This completes the first round of tucks and the splice should look like Figure 36, when viewed from the back. Two more sets of tucks are taken to complete the splice, making three sets in all. For nylon rope, five tucks should be made with each strand. To make the splice bed down smoothly it may be rolled between the palms of the hands or placed on the floor and rolled backwards and forwards a few times with the sole of the foot.

Kicking straps, which are so important to the proper sailing of a dinghy off the wind, should be renewed every season as a matter of course. They are easy and cheap to replace and they have a heavy task to perform.

CHAPTER IV

VARNISH, ENAMEL AND OTHER FINISHES

The ideal finish—Manufacturing processes—Enamels—Undercoats —Primers—Other finishing materials

BEFORE discussing the methods adopted in the preparation of the surface and the application to it of protective and smoothing finishes, it will perhaps be of interest and advantage to describe briefly the most suitable materials which are at our disposal.

The whole range of materials that are likely to be applied to a dinghy hull, in order to achieve a high standard of finish, may be divided into five classes : namely, primers, stoppers, wood fillers, undercoats and finishes. Other materials which will be used, either frequently or occasionally, are thinners and strippers.

The matter does not end here, however, and each class can generally be further sub-divided into many more sections. For instance, apart from a number of different types of paint primers, the priming coat may also be of thinned-down varnish or even a special filler applied directly to the bare wood. Varnish itself is made in a great variety of types which differ widely in their properties of gloss, durability, adhesion, elasticity, toughness, resistance to water absorption and speed of drying. It will be readily understood, then, that there is, or certainly should be, more in the business of varnishing a boat than buying and brushing on a can of varnish (a term which seems to cover a host of products, from those giving superlative finishes of great durability, to those resembling syrup both before and after application).

The wise boat-owner will take the utmost care to obtain the best and most suitable varnish obtainable for his particular job. The finish applied to the hulls and spars of racing dinghies has to stand up to very exacting conditions. In the first place a dinghy hull is fairly flexible and the mast even more so ; consider the rapid vibrations of a racing dinghy's mast when the mainsheet has to be eased completely to hold her upright in a squall. A very hard and brittle coat would quickly crack and flake off such a quaking foundation. Secondly, the racing dinghy helmsman is extremely concerned about keeping the weight of his craft down to the minimum and it is therefor essential that her protective coat absorbs and lets through the least possible amount of moisture, in order that the wood of the planking may not become soaked and heavy. However elastic and shiny a surface may be, it will not be of any use if it becomes impregnated with moisture every time it is immersed. Thirdly, a finish of very high gloss is desired so that the skin friction of the hull may be reduced as much as possible. Fourthly, the finish must be tough enough to withstand the chafe of inhabited trousers sliding over gunwales and the odd knock received from time to time. Fifthly, the adhesion must be good, for there is not much to be gained by using a good finish if it refuses to stay on the surface to which it is applied and peels off like the skin of an over-enthusiastic sun-bather. Finally, it must be fairly easy to apply, reasonably tolerant of the conditions under which it is applied and moderately fast drying ; the ideal conditions for enamelling and varnishing are seldom available when wanted and a slow-drying finish is usually ruined before hardening by specks of dust and flies with suicidal tendencies. There are a lot of other conditions which must be fulfilled—such as paleness in the case of varnish and fastness of colour in the case of enamels—but there is no need to delve deeper into the matter here.

Unmercifully critical of the finish he uses, the dinghy-owner will condemn it if it fails to respond to all the demands made upon it.

It may seem that paint and varnish manufacturers have been presented with a problem which is well-nigh insoluble. In the case of many manufacturers this is doubtless true ; but others, who are constantly investigating new raw materials and processes of manufacture and have the facilities of a staff of expert chemists and physicists experimenting with and testing their products, have gone a long way towards producing the perfect finish. There is no doubt at all that the use of synthetic resins, mainly of the phenol formaldehyde and alkyde types, helps to produce a coat which may be very much superior to the older types which depended on natural resinous substances—such as copal resins, colophony or rosin—to produce a hard glossy surface. Not only is this proved by laboratory tests, but anyone who has had a wide experience of the best of both types can testify to the superiority of those with synthetic rather than natural resinous ingredients, although of course there may be exceptions to the general rule. One of the most useful features of the best of the synthetic varnishes is the fact that the coat dries uniformly throughout its thickness and does not form an initial top skin early in the drying process and remain tacky beneath this for a long while, as the copal varnishes.

A few remarks on the manufacture of synthetic varnish and enamel will perhaps not be out of place here. Since it is one of the ingredients in enamel, let us firstly consider varnish. *Very* roughly the manufacturing process is this : oil, resin, drier and thinner are the ingredients used, the resin being dissolved in the heated oil and cooked with it at a temperature somewhere in the region of 300° C. After this it is cooled somewhat and the thinner and drier added and mixed. This sounds simple enough and one might almost be tempted to try it on the kitchen stove, but it is scarcely necessary to point out that there is a lot more in it than that. Let us look a little more deeply into this wizard's brew.

The oleo-resinous blend is the component of the hard glossy film. It would be a mistake to think that this skin is formed by the mere drying out of volatile thinning agents, for such is not the case ; the oil-resin base does in fact undergo complex chemical, as well as physical, changes during the drying process. The drier is present in minute amounts only and serves only to control and assist the drying-out. The function of the thinner is to suspend the oil-resin base in a chemically and physically inactive condition until it is applied and to maintain it at a suitable consistency for brushing or spraying. The thinner eventually evaporates almost completely from the skin.

Formerly the oily component consisted largely of linseed oil, but this has been almost entirely superseded by other oils providing greater water resistance and increased drying speeds. The kettles in which the highest grades of pale varnish are cooked are cylindrical and constructed of stainless steel and their temperature is under strict technical supervision and sometimes is thermostatically controlled. The hot varnish is constantly stirred by electrically operated stirrers.

After being cooled, the varnish is clarified and filtered by pumping it under great pressure through eight or more separated layers of very thick filter cardboard. Since this process is supposed to eliminate the larger germ microbes, it can have no difficulty in dealing with dust particles or other foreign bodies likely to show in the brushed-out surface. Maturing of the completely processed varnish then takes place in special tanks, after which it is canned and ready for use.

All this sounds fairly simple in itself, but the secret of good varnish does not so much lie in the manufacturing processes which produce it, but the vigilance of the laboratory staff who check every batch of raw material before it is used and are constantly testing the final product. One has only to witness the comparative durability of many brands of varnish, demonstrated by simple weathering tests on varnished planks of wood partially immersed along the side of a pontoon floating in salt water, to realise the vast superiority which this quest for perfection has bestowed upon those brands whose manufacturers seek and have the skill to discover new recipes. One has but to spend a few wearisome hours scraping the inside of a clinker-built hull to be converted with wild enthusiasm, and no thought of the cost, to any varnish the durability of which is superior to its rivals. I feel certain that if the valiant hosts of chemists who are engaged on paint and varnish research could see the bloodshot, dust-filled eyes and the thirsty, lolling tongues of the poor souls who are brave enough to attack the inside of their boats with a scraper to remove poor varnish (whose powers of durability seem barely to exist until the unfortunate being with the scraper tries to get it off !) then they would be encouraged and strengthened in their efforts.

*　　*　　*　　*　　*

Modern enamels consist of pigments ground into varnish and cooked with linseed stand oil and resin. The drier is added on cooling. It will be noted that, once again, the protective coating is largely dependent on the properties of the oleo-resinous blend for its durability. However, other factors to a certain extent govern the lasting qualities of enamels and these may be of interest. Firstly, the pigments themselves must be durable. A few years ago people " in the know " would avoid blues because they tended to fade and chalk or powder ; this disadvantage has now been overcome in the best blue enamels by the substitution of monastral blue in the place of the troublesome pigments previously used. Whites have also been much improved by the adoption of titanium white pigments which provide greater covering power and freedom from excessive powdering. It is of great importance that the covering power of the pigment should be great, for otherwise a large proportion of the pigment has to be used in proportion to the varnish base, thus reducing the amount of that ingredient which confers the properties of durability on the finished enamel. From this point of view, white is not one of the best shades to use if durability is one of the main considerations. Black on the other hand contains a very low proportion of pigment, but, owing to its inability to reflect heat, it gets very hot under the influence of summer suns and this reduces its powers of durability. A medium grey is probably the most durable of all colours. Thus it is seen that considerations of climate should influence not only the choice of type of finish to be used, but even the colour of the finish, if its durability is to be the most important factor ; for while plain black may be the most hardwearing in cold climates, plain white— in spite of the undesirably large proportion of pigment in it—may be the most satisfactory in very hot, sunny climates.

Synthetic resins are also finding their way into the realms of undercoatings and primers, where their properties of tenacity and waterproofness are of the utmost value. Metallic primers have also

47

been used to a considerable extent in recent years, but they cannot be considered an outstanding success because their adhesion to the wood and to the undercoating is relatively poor and flaking off is liable to occur. Metallic aluminium paint does, however, provide a very efficient covering for masts, for the minute overlapping flakes of aluminium lying flat on the wood provide a protective film of very low weight. From the æsthetic point of view, most people will prefer their wooden masts to be varnished.

The function of primers is to seal off the wood to which they are applied and to provide a suitable surface upon which the undercoat can obtain a strong grip. Special primers must be used on metals and these will have anti-corrosive properties for added protection.

Contrary to common belief, the main object behind the use of undercoatings is not to produce a smooth and level surface upon which to apply the final enamel coat, but is to produce a solid ground colour suitable for the finishing coat. Good flowing properties are important in order to reduce rubbing-down to the minimum and the opacity of the coat should be dependent on the quality of the material and not on the thickness of the coats, otherwise much hard work with sandpaper will be necessitated.

In the case of enamelled surfaces, the smooth base to which the final highly glossy coat is applied (which, on a varnished boat, would be built up with successive layers of varnish carefully sandpapered down) should be obtained by the use of a special cement trowelled on over the primer. This material is obtainable in the form of a paste, which is scraped on thinly with a flexible broad-bladed knife, thus filling all small depressions and roughnesses to produce a tough surface which can be sandpapered down with ease to give a smooth coat, providing an excellent key for succeeding layers of under-coating. Its powers of adhesion are good and the drying time is normally from about four to eight hours, according to the thickness of the coat.

Deep depressions in the surface can be filled in with a stopping material. These are obtainable for use under enamels or varnishes and in the latter instance a tinted variety would be used to match the colour of the timber. Stopper can also be used to fill in the deeper scratches caused by wear and tear on the finished surface and should be applied before freshening coats are given. To ensure satisfactory adhesion, the surface should be rubbed down with sandpaper to provide the material with a good keying foundation. (See Chapter I, page 14.) The material will become hard, but is not brittle or likely to chip away under normal conditions.

The most desirable finish for centreboards and rudders is probably provided by an enamel of rather harder finish than that generally used on the hull. In the case of heavy dinghies which have to remain in the water and cannot be brought ashore when not racing, this type of enamel is also suitable for the bottom. Though containing no anti-fouling chemicals, it nevertheless discourages the growth of marine organisms by producing an extremely hard and smooth surface upon which such growths cannot easily gain a foothold. It is also hard enough to stand up satisfactorily to the periodic scrubbings to which small racing boats which are kept afloat will be subjected. Such a finish may be applied direct over the primer coat, since at least two coats should be given and the surface is therefore built up in the same manner as a varnished finish. To obtain the best racing finish, the final coat will be lightly cut down with very fine sandpaper and then burnished or polished to produce a glasslike gloss.

Special deck paints are also manufactured. These are very flexible and able to withstand the working of the deck without cracking, at the same time being hard-wearing. Some manufacturers make a non-slip variety of deck paint which produces a surface rather like sandpaper. This can be a great assistance when working on the decks of small keel boats in a seaway and can be used on the floorboards of dinghies. (See also Chapter IX, page 105.)

In addition to this variety of materials at our disposal, thinners and paint removers will also be used. There is usually a specifically recommended thinning agent for every brand of varnish, enamel or other surface covering, whether protective, smoothing or finishing. Care should be taken to use the type advised or trouble may be experienced when cleaning brushes or diluting coatings. Paint and varnish removers generally consist of a chemical stripper which dissolves the paint film ; in this liquid, which is usually highly volatile and would otherwise quickly evaporate without having time to complete its task, is suspended wax in granular form. The purpose of the wax is to keep the stripper on the job.

Fillers are also made which are intended to be used when the saving of time on the production of a fully-finished varnished surface is important. Such fillers will reduce by several coats the amount of varnish which must be applied and thereby greatly accelerates the completion of the job. A fairly good finish can be obtained in twenty-four hours if this method is used. However, it is not a material which will be utilised to any great extent by those to whom perfection of finish is of more importance than the saving of time, for although it can be tinted to the same colour as the timber on which it is being used, it nevertheless imparts a slightly muddy appearance to it, which will be visible through pale varnish and unsightly at close quarters.

The technique employed in the use of all these materials will be dealt with elsewhere in this book. This chapter seeks merely to familiarise the reader with the materials which are available to him for use on the surfaces of his boat and her spars. Let us now turn our attention to the preparing of the surfaces to which they will be applied.

CHAPTER V

SCRAPING AND SMOOTHING

*Maintaining a good surface—The hull outside—Scraping—Sandpapering—
The hull inside—Cleaning out*

NEW wine should enter sound bottles and new varnish should cling to a sound base. Even if the dinghy owner follows the wise practice of buying only the best for his boat, he will still be disappointed in the results achieved unless the foundation upon which he applies his finishing coat of varnish or enamel is firm and smooth. To those who pass their fingers wonderingly over the mirror-like surface of a perfectly finished dinghy hull and ask the owner—" what do you use to get this finish," the basic answer to the question will probably be—" a dozen sheets of No. o sandpaper every year and the patience and energy required to use it till it's worn out." The best varnish in the world, carefully laid on under perfect conditions, will look wretched unless its foundation is quite smooth. A really first-class base will enable even a poor varnish to produce a reasonable finish.

Alas and alack, careful rubbing down is the principal contributing factor towards the attainment of varnishing perfection and there is no escape. Would that there were, for the task is hard and tedious and one which many would not willingly undertake, were not the reward so great.

Whilst the finish applied to cruising dinghies and other heavier craft, not intended for racing, is meant both to beautify and protect the surface, that which covers the hull of a racing dinghy also serves the further purposes of reducing water absorption and skin friction. The beautifying and protection of the hull is probably of secondary importance to the out-and-out racing man, who might suffer his boat to be painted in dazzling checks or gaudy stripes regardless of all sense of beauty, if he thought that thereby her speed would be increased by a fraction ; the necessary protection can be afforded by careful attention to boat covers and the conditions under which the dinghy is kept. It is rather doubtful if a superfine finish does in fact increase the speed of a dinghy much in light weather, but there is no doubt at all that, all other things being equal (they seldom are), a boat with a really smooth under-water surface will have a slight advantage over one with an average finish. This being the case, no racing dinghy owner can afford to ignore the small benefit which hard work with sandpaper and paint brush can give her.

A racing hull which is properly cared for is very little trouble to keep in good order. Once the condition has been allowed to deteriorate, then the hard work commences. The surest way to save yourself trouble later on, in the case of a varnished hull, is never to allow the weather or water to get into a bare patch of wood from which the finish has been chipped or worn. A little varnish should be put on such places immediately they are noticed, even if it is not possible to smooth the surface down or allow the varnish to dry properly before the boat is sailed. Such first-aid patches, which are mentioned in Chapter 1 but deserve to be re-emphasised, will at least afford protection to the wood and prevent it from being discoloured ; and even though the varnish may collect some whiskers from the fluffy sweater of your crew or a few pock-marks from the spray, it can be rubbed down at a later date with far less effort than would be involved in scraping out a discoloured patch of wood.

There is no real reason why a racing dinghy should not look in as good condition when she is ten years old as when she is quite new, providing proper care is taken of her. It may necessitate the sacrifice of a few days' sailing during the course of a year, but I believe this to be worth while.

However, let us deal with a dinghy which has been allowed to get into a shocking condition. That no one's feelings may be hurt, let us imagine that she has been bought cheaply second-hand and has not been allowed to get in to that state by anyone reading this book !

We are faced by two alternatives : either we can botch the job up a bit and just rub down the places where the finish is obviously decayed and liable to chip and peel off, adding two or three coats of varnish over the whole hull ; or else we can scrape the entire hull down to the bare wood. The latter is the correct choice and will pay handsome dividends in the long run. Since you are only reading about it and do not, I hope, actually have to do it, you will presumably not grudge a little space being devoted to this brave task. For the sake of an example we will deal with the ancient and neglected hull of an *International 14-foot* dinghy.

Before we get down to the job, it may be as well to alleviate to some extent the mental suffering which may have been caused to the reader by my comments concerning the horrors of scraping. It *is* a fairly formidable task and not one which would be recommended as an altogether entertaining occupation, but the revival of a sadly neglected boat which hovers habitually near the tail of the racing fleet and the conversion of her into a fresh and sparkling race-winner, is a task which has many compensations and thrills. Moreover,

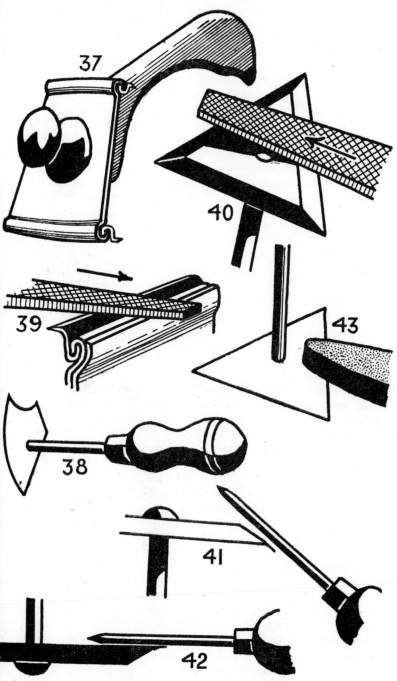

Figures 37, 38, 39, 40, 41, 42 and 43

regarding the question from a purely financial viewpoint, the value of a racing dinghy can be almost doubled by a really skilful resuscitation. It would be a mistake to belittle the magnitude of the operation, for that might encourage carelessness in everyday maintenance with the belief that everything can be put right in a few hours by an afternoon's scraping. Some may even be tempted to apply exceptionally thick and heavy coats of varnish in an effort to take short cuts to final finishes on the recommendations of knowing individuals who lightheartedly (one is tempted to say light-headedly) tell them that " it can all be easily scraped off, if you overdo it and it runs a bit." By way of encouragement, let me add that I have scraped four dinghies that I have owned in the past dozen years and have found that in each case it was well worth while.

The job should be tackled under cover so that the bared wood will not be exposed to the weather. If it is not possible to find a building in which to carry out the whole process, a good tarpaulin should be spread over the hull to keep it dry after the day's scraping has been done. It is wise to lay the tarpaulin on battens so that it is lifted off the hull, otherwise condensation on the underside of the tarpaulin may damp the wood of the planking.

The hull is first chocked-up at a convenient height so that the worker's back is not bent into too uncomfortable a curve. The tools used are a scraper, stripping material and, occasionally, a wire brush. Scrapers may be obtained in a variety of different types, the more modern type of hook scraper probably being the best for amateurs, though professionals often use ancient and bloodthirsty-looking weapons and even pieces of broken glass. Hook scrapers usually have detachable blades which may be renewed or sharpened quite easily. There are a number of different shapes and sizes of hook scraper. One with a fairly wide and slightly curved blade, as in Figure 37, will be the most useful and a small heart-shaped or combination heart-shaped and triangular scraper of the older type, seen in Figure 38, will be very handy for getting into difficult corners.

One of the main essentials to remember when scraping is to keep the tool very sharp. Every five or ten minutes is not too frequent for attention to the blade with a sharpening stone or fine, keen file. Not only will you be able to cut the old varnish away with less effort and wasted time, but the periodic sharpening causes a break in the scraping operations which relieves the tedium of the job and allows the attack to be recommenced with renewed vigour. Furthermore blunt scrapers arouse savage instincts in those who handle them and are apt to encourage tearing away at the surface by pure brute force, with the result that the scraper will probably skid off at an angle and produce deep furrows in the planking.

54

Slippery hulls, creaseless sails and a catlike smoothness of movement on the part of helmsman and crew do much to win races on days such as this. *National 12's* and *Fireflies* are seen racing together at Henley.

The makers of some hook scrapers now also sell very neat little sharpening stones with handles which are specially made for keeping the blades of their scrapers keen. The job can, of course, be done with an ordinary sharpening stone, but these special ones are easily slipped into the pocket and are therefore handy at all times. Little need be said about the sharpening of hook scrapers, except that the angle of the cutting edge should be kept constant and, of course, the direction of travel of the sharpening stone or file over the hook is towards the cutting edge as in Figure 39.

The older type of size scraper depends on an artificially produced burr for its efficiency. The blade is first filed as in Figure 40, care being taken to see that the edges remain flat and even. After this the burr is produced easily, by rubbing a brad-awl along the bevelled surface, as in Figure 41, which also shows the burr. This burr is then bent so that it is a continuation of the flat side of the scraper ; this is done by rubbing the brad-awl along the flat surface. Figure 42 shows this being done and will also give an idea of the resulting burr. Fairly strong pressure should be maintained on the awl while making and manipulating this burr.

Sometimes it may be found preferable to have a cutting edge on the scraper, particularly when working across the grain. This can best be produced by using a sharpening stone, firstly in the manner described in the previous paragraph on filing up an edge and secondly by moving it back and forth across the flat surface of the back of the scraper, as in Figure 43.

* * * * *

There are several methods of undermining the resistance of varnish, but only one which can be really recommended, that being the use of varnish stripper or remover. Burning off with a blowlamp is sometimes the method adopted on painted boats and treatment with hot caustic soda is also employed on occasion, but neither of them are practices which are to be recommended to the racing dinghy owner and the latter is dangerous to the hands and will cause burns on the face if splashing occurs. If caustic soda is used it must be neutralised before any varnish is applied to the wood with a solution of vinegar—one part vinegar to four parts of water—and well rinsed with water (it is as well to test the surface with litmus paper which can be obtained from any chemist—it goes red for acids and blue for alkalis).

Varnish remover should be applied to a small area at a time with an old brush. Once the volatile solvent has evaporated its value is lost and it will do no more towards the softening of the varnish. This is a generalisation which may not apply to all types of strippers and in any case the instructions of individual manufacturers should always be followed.

Techniques in the handling of strippers no doubt vary considerably and are largely dictated by the nature of the stripper used. I generally find it best to operate on two portions of the surface at a time. An explanation of my system is this. First of all the length of time for which the solvent remains liquid and doing its job of softening the varnish is established by experience; the time taken for the solvent to soften the maximum thickness of varnish is also discovered. Obviously it will be best to scrape it and the softened varnish off between these two times. Let us, for the sake of argument, say that the solvent evaporates from the job after fifteen minutes and has softened the varnish as deeply as it will in five minutes. The scraping should therefore be done in the ten minutes between these two times and an area no greater than can be scraped comfortably in five minutes should be treated with the stripper. Referring to

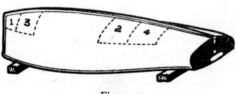

Figure 44

Figure 44, the stripper would first of all be applied to the area 1; this will take about two and a half minutes. Another two and a half minutes are spent sharpening the scraper, so that five minutes altogether will have elapsed between the commencement of the application of stripper to area 1, and the commencement of the application to area 2. Scraping is then started in area 1, until as much as possible of the softened varnish has been removed, when the attention is turned to area 2, which is scraped until it is in a similar condition. The process is repeated on areas 3 and 4—and so on. The softened varnish is in this way never allowed time to harden up again, whilst the stripper is never scraped off until it has had time to do as much as it is likely to in the way of dissolving the varnish. If the job is done thus, no time, energy or stripper is wasted.

Thick and old coverings of varnish will require two, three or even four applications of stripper before they are completely removed, each layer of softened varnish being scraped off between applications. If this is the case, I prefer not to stick to the two original areas until they are completely done, but to make one application to the entire boat, divided into areas, before making a second application to any one place. The reason for this is that otherwise large expanses of bare wood are exposed for a long time and are very liable to get splashed or even saturated with stripper while the other portions are being dealt with ; this means more work later on to kill, or render ineffective, the stripper which has soaked into the wood, for otherwise succeeding coats of varnish will be destroyed and lifted off.

The height at which the boat is arranged is most important from the point of view of comfort and efficiency when scraping. If she is up too high, it is very hard to exert a suitable pressure on the scraper, while if she is too low, the pangs of backache will soon make themselves felt. For this reason I believe it best to arrange the successive areas to which the stripper is applied in rows along the length of the boat and to do the row next to the keel on both sides before starting on a row nearer to the gunwale. The boat can then be raised or lowered between rows and so be kept at the most convenient height for the worker.

Great care should be taken not to scrape too deeply. The woodwork itself should never be scraped away, but only the covering upon it. The skins of the planking of many dinghies are very thin and cannot suffer much reduction. Furthermore, if the level of the wood is scraped away so as to leave the nail heads raised, the latter must be cut down with a file to leave a smooth surface ; this may mean cutting away a considerable amount of the nail head, which was probably also reduced appreciably after the hull was planked up during building. Result—a weakened hull with paper-thin nail heads.

If the gunwales are badly stained and weathered, they can well stand a thin sliver of wood being taken off them without the hull being weakened in any way. In this case the method to be recommended is to remove all the varnish with a scraper and then cut down the wood slightly with a sharp, fine-set, smoothing plane, which will cut away the wood far more cleanly than will a paint scraper. As an alternative to planing, a cabinet maker's panel scraper may be used. This is simply a flat saw-steel plate and is remarkably effective, providing it is kept properly keen and is used correctly.

There are three stages in producing a properly sharpened panel scraper. As in the case of size scrapers, the work is done by a burr which is turned over so as to be at an effective cutting angle to the wood. The first stage is to produce carefully squared edges to the scraper with the aid of a fine flat file ; this is, of course, done by filing along rather than across the edge. Figure 45 shows the way it is done. The burr is then produced by rubbing with a bradawl as previously described in the case of the size scraper. The bradawl is held so that its blade or shaft lies at a very shallow angle to

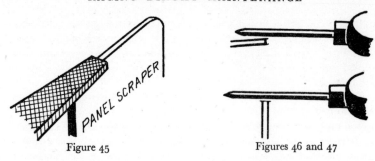

Figure 45   Figures 46 and 47

the surface of the scraper and the burr produced is as in Figure 46. This burr is then turned over by rubbing with the brad-awl along the edge. Figure 47 shows how this is done and the final burr which it is desired to produce.

Any patches of weathered wood which cannot be scraped or planed out, can frequently be bleached successfully with a warm solution of oxalic acid. The acid should be applied to the dark patches with an old brush and it should not be allowed to get into contact with the clothes or fingers ; it is a *deadly poison*. Several liberal applications may be needed to badly weathered spots and the acid should be allowed a day or two to dry out between treatments. After the bleaching has been successfully accomplished, the area to which the acid has been applied should be well washed with methylated spirit.

Before filing flat any nail heads which have been accidentally raised by the too deep scraping of the wood around them, precautions should be taken to " kill " any traces of stripper which may remain on the hull. The manufacturers of the stripping agent generally issue instructions on how best to do this and frequently it is done by wiping over with a rag soaked in turpentine. This is a most important procedure, for not only will new varnish be lifted off the wood by any traces of the active solvent which may remain in the timber, but also the wax base, which is a constituent of many strippers, will prevent the adherence of any finish. Do not attempt to rub down the nail heads or sandpaper the woodwork until the turpentine has dried away, otherwise your file and sandpaper will be quickly clogged and the softened wood will be torn away instead of being cut down cleanly.

A wide flat file should be used when dealing with the raised nail heads and, if possible, a new one which is fine-toothed, but sharp, should be used. Old and blunted files will not bite into the metal properly and tend to wear down the softer wood around the nail before they can be induced to complete a decent job on the harder nail head itself. If any nail heads are depressed below the surface, preventing the scraper from getting to them, the varnish should be picked off them with a knife, for it will have been attacked by the stripper and if allowed to remain will eventually lift off, taking any covering of new varnish with it. The same applies to traces of varnish left in screw head slots or in the angle between the lands of the planking of clinker-built boats ; all these nooks and crannies must be well cleared of any softened varnish.

The hull should now be smoothed off with sandpaper. Any badly roughened places can be cut down with Middle 2 grade, but Fine 2 grade is quite coarse enough for the general surface. When finishing off, rub with the grain, not across it.

If varnish is to be applied, the hull can now be stained if it is considered desirable. A spirit stain should be used as this will not raise the grain to the same extent as the variety which is dissolved in water. The stain should be applied with a rag to get an even colour and should be allowed to dry thoroughly before any varnishing is commenced. Stained hulls sometimes create suspicion in the purchasers of older boats, probably because of the fear that staining may be an attempt to hide some defects ; it cannot really do this, but the point should be borne in mind if it is intended to sell the boat in the near future.

The processes involved in removing enamel or paint are similar to those already described for varnish, except that there will be no necessity to bleach weathered areas of wood. In spite of the fact that the wood may be discoloured by the weather, it is probably quite sound and, so long as the grain is properly smoothed with sandpaper, it can be completely hidden by any opaque pigmented finish.

If paintwork is being scraped off and is to be varnished instead of repainted, difficulty may be experienced in removing the paint completely from the grain of the wood. A fine wire brush may be used for this job. The surface is first scraped so that the majority of the paint is removed, leaving only that in the soft grain of the wood. A fresh dose of stripper is then applied and, after the usual softening up period, the surface is scrubbed in the direction of the grain with the wire brush. This method inevitably roughens the surface somewhat by wearing away the soft wood ; careful sandpapering will restore the smoothness and, unless the boat is unfortunate enough to be constantly changing hands from one owner who likes varnish to another who prefers enamel, it is not a process which she will have to undergo more than once.

* * * * *

The inside of the hull is a rather more serious task than the outside, especially in the case of a clinker-built boat. All but those with considerable time available should think twice before embarking on the job of getting a clinker-built boat down to the bare wood, for the results obtained may not always justify the labour involved. Not to discourage, but to forewarn the enthusiast, it would seem wise to stress the practical difficulties. It should be pointed out that the following snags apply only to clinker-built boats with ribs ; a few of the most modern clinker hulls are being constructed without ribs and without nail fastenings, the lands of the planking being glued and in some cases screwed. These boats are almost as easy to scrape inside as outside but, being so much easier to keep in good condition, should never need scraping any way. There is a snag to this type of construction, however, for the planks are liable to split at the overlap.

The difficulties involved in the interior scraping of a normal clinker hull are caused by the ribs and the rooves over which the plank nails are riveted on the inside. The fact that the ribs prohibit the free use of the scraper along the lengths of the planks, and necessitate working across the planks at right angles to the grain of the wood, means that there is grave danger of tearing away the soft wood in the grain and causing ridges over the harder wood of the grain. Furthermore, the rooves and riveted nail heads cause an obstruction even to scraping across the grain, so that, generally speaking, some obstruction or other is being encountered most of the time. However, patience and a small and handy scraper may be able to overcome these difficulties. But there is, unfortunately, one other snag which is most difficult to surmount : unless extreme care is taken, the stripper will soften the varnish in the gap between the underside of the ribs and the upper plank at the overlap of two planks, as in Figure 48. This

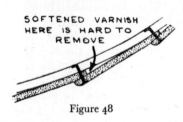

SOFTENED VARNISH HERE IS HARD TO REMOVE

Figure 48

softened varnish may be well-nigh impossible to remove, with the result that the new varnish will have to be applied over the top of a weakened foundation. Moreover, this undesirable state of affairs is existent in a situation in which it is especially desirable to have good protection, for the water lodges there and moisture is retained amongst the grit and fluff which are liable to accumulate in such places.

To those brave souls who tackle the task, I would recommend the use of an old hacksaw blade for getting right into the crevices beneath the ribs. One of these old blades bent over and sharpened like a hook scraper makes a very handy little tool for getting into tricky corners.

Having scraped and sandpapered all or part of the inside, it is necessary to clean out all the grit and dust before any attempt is made to apply any varnish or enamel. If the hull is undecked, the job is an easy one, for it can be turned upside down and set up on high trestles while the interior is dusted out with a brush, great care being taken to see that no dust is allowed to remain on the undersides (upper sides, when the boat is upside down) of the thwarts, gunwales, etc., otherwise this will simply fall back into the bottom when she is righted. It is as well to put on an old cap or something to prevent most of last season's accumulation of seaweed and shingle getting into your hair.

If the boat is decked the job is rather harder, for the dust will be trapped by it. A vacuum cleaner of the cylinder type is, of course, the best solution to the problem, but even if one is available and diplomacy is successful in winning it from its domestic spheres for a little while, the electric power is not always available for the working of it. In the case of a boat with fore and side decks only, and no deck aft, which has to be dusted out without the aid of a vacuum cleaner, probably the best way is to stand her on her tail as in Figure 49. Adequate padding should be pro-

vided so that the weight of the boat is not taken by the rudder hangings and she should be secured upright by tying guys to her stemhead and securing them well out at an angle; three should be sufficient. This method necessitates the use of a long-handled brush or a step-ladder to deal with the raised bow of the boat, but if care is taken to clear the dust off the upper (bow) sides of the ribs and any other flat surfaces normally facing the bow, it is an efficient way of cleaning out.

If the boat is entirely decked there are two ways of doing the job in a more or less satisfactory manner without a vacuum cleaner. The first is to sweep all the dust towards the keel and then remove as

Figure 49

much of it as possible with a damped rag. A good deal of dust will remain in the bottom of the boat, but the sides, thwarts, side benches and so on will be clean and these can be varnished and allowed to dry. The hull is then turned upside down and the dust which remains by the keel can, to a great extent, be brushed out ; that which remains will fall on to the newly varnished sides, but will do them no harm since they will by this time be dry. The bottom of the hull inside—the parts nearest to the keel—can now be varnished with the boat upside down and allowed to dry before it is righted. The snag about this method is that it is difficult to varnish the inside when the dinghy is upside down and some form of lighting is essential under the boat while the job is being done. On the other hand a dust-free finish is obtainable.

The other method of dealing with a decked boat, is to sweep all the dirt towards the keel, as in the former case, and remove as much of it as possible with a damp cloth. The remaining dust is carefully swept as near as possible to the keel. Damp cloths are then laid over the keel and garboard strakes (those planks nearest the keel) to keep any remaining dirt from blowing about. The inside of the hull is then varnished to one plank above the garboard strake and allowed to dry, whereupon the cloths are removed. The small amount of dust at the keel and garboard is then swept away from the keel and up the planking on to the newly dried varnish. The cloths are then once more laid down over the dust and the two planks nearest the keel, on either side, and the keel or hogpiece itself are varnished.

Both of the two foregoing methods are adopted on the principle that, whereas dust and grit remaining on the surface to be varnished are ruinous to the finish and produce a poor surface which is very hard to rectify, a little bit of dust swept up over new varnish already properly dried, has no adverse effect on the finish and it is, in fact, a normal and almost unavoidable state of affairs, to have a little dirt in the bottom of a dinghy. They are neither of them counsels of perfection—only the vacuum cleaner can produce perfect cleanliness inside the hull—but they are both practical methods of producing surfaces for finishing, if not a perfectly dusted boat.

CHAPTER VI

APPLYING VARNISH

*Dusting off—First coats—Clinker hulls—Carvel hulls—Storing varnish—
Brushing technique—Care of brushes—Second and third coats—Rubbing
down—Fourth and fifth coats—Anti-dust precautions—Final coats—
Some " don'ts "*

T HE techniques employed in producing finished enamelled and
varnished surfaces are widely different. Let us first deal with
varnishing.

The bare wood hull is arranged upside down at a convenient
height—generally with the gunwales raised about a foot or eighteen
inches off the ground. Not only does this make it less tiring for the
worker and easier for him to see the job properly, but it also helps
to keep the gunwales and top strakes free from dust stirred up or
blown off the floor.

It is most unwise to attempt to varnish (or enamel) in the open
air. Besides the fact that grit, dust, flies, grass seed, leaves and butter-
flies will almost certainly find the wet surface an irresistible attrac-
tion, the chance of raindrops descending upon the still tacky surface
and ruining it with pockmarks is too great, in this country at any
rate, to make the gamble a fair one. Make the utmost endeavour to
have a good roof over the job. However, at this stage in the pro-
ceedings it is neither essential nor really desirable to devote much
time towards producing really dust-proof conditions by erecting
dust sheets over and around the boat or by any other complicated
method. During the rubbing down stages the worker is bound to
create so much dust which will fly about and cling to the dust sheets,
later falling with evil consequences on to the final and all-important
coat and spoiling it, that, unless he is prepared to remove and shake
the dust sheets between every coat which is applied to the hull,
they are better not used till the last two coats.

The hull must, of course, be dusted off before any varnish is
applied and this should be done immediately before the commencement of each actual application—not half an hour before so that,
during the time before the varnishing begins, further downfalls of
dust have settled on the surface to be covered.

The correct atmosphere in which to apply varnish is one which is
clean and dry and at a temperature of about 60°F.

The first coat of varnish should be thinned-down with twenty per cent of the thinning agent recommended by the manufacturers of the varnish being used. Most manufacturers make special thinners for their own varnish recipe and, just as one man's poison is another man's meat, one varnish's thinner may be another's coagulating ruin—don't add a remaining odd spot of " Shino " thinner to " Glosso " varnish. It is most important to stir the thinner into the varnish—not vice versa ; pour in a little at a time and keep stirring. If a great dollop of thinner is added in, or the varnish added to the thinner, the setting process of a synthetic varnish may be upset and bits of prematurely set varnish may be precipitated ; these will float around as hard little chips in the mixture and later cause noticeable specks in the dried varnish.

The thinned varnish should be applied fairly liberally and will mostly soak into the absorbent timber. Most birch plywoods, mahoganys and teaks will absorb more than will oak and ash. It is advisable not to apply more varnish than will comfortably soak into the timber leaving the surface quite free from semi-glossy and tacky varnish. The wood will, of course, be brightened and changed in colour by the varnish, but no trace of wet varnish should remain visible upon it.

Clinker-built boats should be varnished along the lengths of the planks. Start at the keel at either bow or stern and work along this and the garboard strake to the other end. Then, commencing the next plank at the same end from which the preceding plank was first tackled, proceed to the other end of this one. And so on, with succeeding planks to the gunwale. Figure 50 will explain the method. One side of the boat is done at a time.

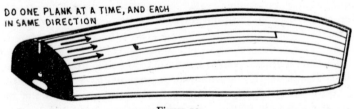

DO ONE PLANK AT A TIME, AND EACH IN SAME DIRECTION

Figure 50

If the shed or room in which the varnishing is being done is very dirty, it may be advisable to clean off the planking as the varnishing is being done, though it should scarcely be necessary during the first coat unless the conditions are very bad. While there is any wet or tacky varnish about, the dusting brush should not be used, for it flicks the dirt about too much ; nor should woollen or fluffy ma-

66

terial be used for a duster. When cleaning dust off a bare wood surface, use a non-fluffy cotton rag which has been moistened with a fifty-fifty mixture of varnish and thinners ; the dust particles will stick to this slightly tacky cloth and they will be removed. Do not dust off the plank adjacent to that to which you have just applied varnish, but always dust two planks ahead of any which are still tacky, otherwise there is a good chance of disturbing dirt on to the sticky surface. The rag should never be used to flick dust off, but should rather be smoothly and carefully wiped over the surface.

Personally, I dust off the plank two ahead of the one which I have just varnished as a matter of routine, whether the air appears to be dusty or not, as I find that it makes a desirable break in the actual varnishing. Once the varnishing of one side has been commenced, it should be continued to its conclusion without delay. This is not so important in the case of a first coat, but certainly is with building-up and finishing coats. The reason is that, with a modern fast-drying varnish, it will not be found possible to " join-up " fresh varnish to that which has already become partly dried, for the more recent application will not intermingle and flow into that which is tacky and well advanced in the setting process.

Carvel-built and smooth-skinned hulls should be varnished in narrow strips from keel to gunwale in order that no difficulty in joining-up may be encountered. Figure 51 shows how the hull is divided up for the varnishing process. First of all you should varnish along the keel and garboard strake for about eighteen inches ; then grad-

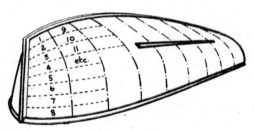

Figure 51

ually work down the planking, parallel to the keel in strips of the same length till the gunwale is reached. Then return to the keel and, with the next strip of eighteen inches width, continue in the same manner. In this way the freshly applied varnish is only required to join up with varnish which has been applied perhaps six or seven minutes earlier, when the corresponding area of the preceding strip was covered, and there should be no unsightly brush marks or lack of proper flow between the strips. For a fast-drying varnish the strips should be narrower than for a slow-drying varnish ; similarly the strips can be wider in cool weather than they would be in hot and arid conditions. Because the surface distance from keel to gunwale is far greater about amidships, the strips towards the midship section of the hull should be narrower than those towards the ends, for each area will take longer to cover.

Generally speaking, I think that it will be found easier to varnish in the direction opposite to the hand in which the brush is normally held. That is to say that if the brush is held in the right hand, then the varnishing will be done from right to left when viewed by the person wielding the brush. In this way you will never be leaning over the work that you have just done and breathing on it or waving fluffy cloths menacingly above it. Furthermore you will be looking at it from an angle from which it will be far easier to see if you have covered all the surface and to judge whether you have brushed it out smoothly.

The varnish (or enamel) should never be used directly from the can, but a little should be decanted into a spotlessly clean glass jar or tin. The reason for this is obvious, for if the varnish is taken straight from the can, it means that the latter must be left unstoppered throughout the time that it takes to apply its entire contents, with the result that the prolonged exposure to the air will undoubtedly start the drying process in the can and the fluid varnish will be filled with prematurely hardened specks. Furthermore, the frequent dipping of the brush into the can will almost certainly deposit into the varnish specks of dust, which are bound to be picked up from the surface of the boat in spite of all precautions to remove it beforehand.

Where the bottle or tin into which the brush is dipped, should be placed, is itself something of a problem. On no account should it be placed so that a brush loaded with varnish has to pass over the surface already covered, otherwise there is a danger of drips falling on to it and eventually drying out into wrinkled blobs which will ruin the surface. It is less serious if the drips fall on to a surface which has yet to be varnished, but it is nevertheless undesirable and they should be avoided if possible ; if they should occur, they should be wiped off before drying with a cotton rag moistened with thinners and varnish in a fifty-fifty proportion. It is not wise to rest the tin on the bottom planking, for it is almost certain to have dust and grime adhering to it which will be deposited on the hull. Nor is it advisable to put it on the floor, where dust is so liable to be blown or stirred up into it. The best thing to do is to wrap a cloth around it to prevent drips from falling down its sides and to hold it in one hand ; failing this, put it on a box by the side of the boat and slide the box along as you work from one end to the other.

I always decant, immediately, every fresh can of varnish that I buy into perfectly clean small bottles of about sufficient size to do one side of the hull. I fill the bottles to the brim, stopper them and store them at an even temperature in the dark. This ensures that the varnish will not expand in hot weather and push the corks out and I believe that darkness helps to keep the varnish in a pale condition (this belief may now be out of date). In this way there is always the certainty of having perfectly fresh varnish quite free from the bits and skin which are normally encountered when using a partially emptied can in which—however well stoppered—there is sufficient air to permit the drying of the varnish to a limited degree. If you do not bother to do this, always seal your varnish can in the following manner :—when putting the lid on, squeeze the sides of the can to drive out as much air as possible, then push the lid well home and turn the can upside down for a moment to seal in the lid with varnish. This method will ensure that the lid will not loosen in hot weather when the contents of the can will expand and would try to force the lid off, were it not for the fact that as much air as possible is expressed from the can before it is sealed.

The brush should not be dipped deeply into the varnish or overloaded. About three-eighths of an inch depth of varnish along the bottom edge of the brush is quite sufficient. Always apply a freshly loaded brush to the *higher* part of the area which you expect it to cover ; in this way the varnish will flow downwards under the action of gravity and will help the brushing out process to produce an evenly thick film.

Figure 52 will help to explain this. Do not allow any accumulation of varnish to collect in the angle between the planks of a clinker boat or this will dry out crinkly.

It is not a good thing to fiddle with varnish once it is on, but great

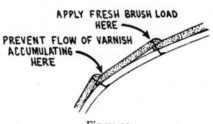

APPLY FRESH BRUSH LOAD HERE

PREVENT FLOW OF VARNISH ACCUMULATING HERE

Figure 52

care should be taken to see that it is brushed out evenly, otherwise the thicker patches will run or " pull " and produce wrinkles or " weeps " over the surface. It should be brushed on with longitudinal strokes in the direction of the planking, crossed off with transverse strokes to ensure even spreading, and finally smoothed out very carefully with feather-light longitudinal strokes with the tip of the brush.

Varnish and enamel brushes should always be of the best quality obtainable and a good one is worth taking care of. The bristles should be firmly anchored and should not come adrift when the brush is in use. Many varieties of different brushes are used, but the inexperienced will probably find that a flat two-inch brush with fine bristles set in rubber will be the most satisfactory for him. The bristles should be tapered toward the tip as in Figure 53. New brushes should be soaked for a few days in water before being used ; this will soften the bristles and will set them firmly in place. The brush may be suspended in the pot of water by a wire or nail pushed through the hole shown in Figure 53 ; this may rest on the

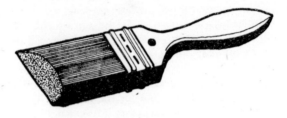

Figure 53

rim of the jar. After soaking, the metal band of the brush should be tapped on the angle of the edge of a bench or board ; this will flick the water out from the bristles and will also dislodge any loose bristles which may then be picked out.

Varnish brushes used for applying synthetic finishes should be rinsed out after use in a mixture of fifty per cent varnish and thinners. They should then be further rinsed in a fifty per cent mixture of thinners and linseed oil and kept suspended in this mixture. This is most important, for any attempts to wash out with one hundred per cent thinners will result in the precipitation of chips of artificially hardened varnish which will be very difficult to remove from the brush before it is next used. The brushes should be supported so that the bristles do not touch the bottom of the vessel in which they are stored.

When varnishing a clinker hull, the transom is best left till last because, in any case, it will be impossible to join it up evenly with either side. With a carvel hull, however, if the first side to be done is commenced from the bows and worked towards the stern, the transom can then be done and finally the other side, which will be varnished from the stern towards the bow. Thus, if we consider a right-handed person adopting the method of working from right to left as detailed on page 68, he will commence on the port bow and continue along the port side and right round the hull until he reaches the stem again. Any difficulty in joining up will thereby be eliminated.

Having applied the first thinned coat of varnish, the hull should be allowed about twelve hours to dry—some varnishes will take longer. A second coat, this time of unthinned varnish, can then be applied without any preliminary rubbing down, as the first coat will have soaked right into the wood and will give an excellent keying surface on which to build succeeding coats.

The second coat is allowed at least thirty hours to dry and is then *lightly* rubbed down with No. 1 sandpaper. I prefer to use an ordinary sandpaper dry at this stage, as wet rubbing down with waterproof sandpaper might raise the grain if the very thin varnish layer was worn through to the bare wood in some places. The purpose of rubbing down at this stage is to remove from the surface any small whiskers of wood which previously escaped being sandpapered off because they were too flexible ; now, however, they will be supported and stiffened by the varnish and will easily be shaved off.

The third coat of varnish is applied moderately thickly and allowed plenty of time to dry out.

*　　*　　*　　*　　*

We now have the basis upon which the smooth surface is built up and the third coat should produce a good gloss which will reveal the fact that, although you may have thought the hull to be very even, it is in fact covered with little bumps and hollows.

The continued applications of varnish and cutting down with sandpaper will fill in the hollows and rub off the bumps. In this lies the whole secret of producing a first-class surface. There are no satisfactory short cuts and it is most unwise to be tempted into trying any. Some people recommend putting on very thick coats of varnish to build up the surface quickly, but this is a very dangerous procedure likely to lead to highly unsatisfactory results or even the ruinous catastrophe which demands further work with the scraper. Wood fillers are made for use under varnish and with the aid of these a reasonable finish can be obtained with three coats of varnish, but, as was mentioned in Chapter IV, the results are not really up to the standard required for a racing dinghy and the filler produces a muddy appearance under the varnish ; however, durability is not diminished and the time taken to produce a full finish is remarkably short.

The object of rubbing down is twofold. The prime reason is to smooth down the surface. It is scarcely necessary to point out that a glossy surface is not necessarily a smooth one and it is probably correct to say that a smooth surface is of considerably more importance, where skin friction is concerned, than is gloss. Figure 54, which represents enlarged cross-sections through timber at various stages in the varnishing process, will help to show how ridges can appear in the varnish over woodwork that was perfectly smooth in its bare state, as at (*a*). At (*b*) one coat of thinned varnish has been

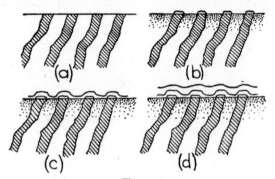

Figure 54

applied ; this has soaked deeply into the soft wood of the timber, but to a smaller extent into the hard wood of the grain upon which it has formed a thin film and dried. The second coat also soaks into the soft wood to a slight degree and builds up still more over the first coat film on the hard grain, as at (*c*), making the ridges more pronounced. The third coat tends to flow off the ridges and fill the hollows and this begins to smooth out the surface as shown at (*d*). The action of sandpaper on such a surface needs no explanation and is simply to cut down the humps.

The humps and hollows are not only caused by the texture of the wood. For instance fastenings may depress the surface of the timber around them, while a nick in the plane of the boat-builder or timber yard may make a little ridge on both sides of every plank. The cleverly built-up surface can nullify or hide a multitude of petty sins.

The second reason for patient rubbing down is to produce a good base or " keying surface " on which to apply succeeding coats of varnish. A new varnish coat will not cling with any tenacity to a surface which is highly glossy and it must therefore be sanded down to a matt surface upon which the new coat can get a firm foothold. Where a smooth, flat surface is already in existence and a coat is being applied simply to freshen up the gloss, some people prefer not to sandpaper to produce the keying surface. However, rubbing down wet with waterproof sandpaper is probably the best method of flatting the surface or producing a properly keyed base, though in the latter case a very fine grade, such as 400A, should be used. Other materials used for getting a keyed surface are steel wool, pumice powder and similar common abrasives. Steel wool does the

It is in this sort of weather that concert-pitch tuning is probably of the greatest importance. Strong winds try the strength of gear and faint airs the patience and alertness of crews, but when a comfortable little breeze is driving a racing dinghy along, minute adjustments to the boat and her gear may play a major part as a race-winning factor.

job quickly, but very great care must be taken to remove all the small bits of metal which will break off and lodge most cunningly in cracks and crevices, later causing unsightly rust marks under the varnish if they are allowed to remain : the net saving of time by using steel wool is therefore reduced to nil by the extra time which has to be spent in dusting off.

But to return to the question of rubbing down for the purposes of flattening the surface. The sandpaper should, whenever possible, be of the waterproof type known as " wet or dry," or simply " W.O.D." The most satisfactory grade to use is 1/2, though a slightly coarser grade could be used if the surface is poor and a quicker job is required. It should be used wet, with a little soap. Used thus, the abrasive will grind down the surface and will not scratch or simply rub it away. If W.O.D. paper cannot be obtained, ordinary sandpaper of Fine 2 grade should be used. When rubbing down with a dry sandpaper do not press too hard and do not rub away too long at any one place ; if one spot needs a lot of rubbing down, come back to it at intervals between doing the rest of the surface, otherwise the continued friction over a small area will generate so much heat that the varnish will peel off unevenly and clog the sandpaper, which may then scratch the surface deeply and badly. Never continue to use sandpaper which has become clogged or blunted, for it may scar the surface badly and it will take a long time to achieve very little in the way of de-ridging. It will probably take from eight to ten sheets of sandpaper to rub down a 14-foot hull properly each time.

The most effective way to use sandpaper is to fold and tear each sheet, across its length, into two : then fold each half over three times, as shown in Figure 55. It will be seen that one rough surface is in contact with the smooth underside of the upper layer ; this prevents one layer from slipping on the other and makes a firm pad. The flat of the hand should be used to move and exert slight pressure on the pad of sandpaper. Cork or other sandpapering blocks are not very satisfactory. The sandpaper should frequently be lifted

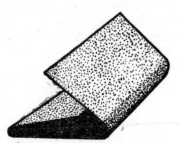

Figure 55

up and slapped on the surface being rubbed down, to remove the varnish dust from both the paper and the planking ; this will much reduce the tendency of the paper towards clogging.

* * * * *

To continue with our building up of a final surface. The coats already applied are cut down fairly well, but care must be taken not to rub down to the bare wood anywhere. After rubbing down, the hull should be carefully looked over and any deep scratches, depressed nail heads, or old battle scars should be filled in and smoothed with a coloured stopper. A stopper with good powers of adhesion should be used, for it is expected to remain in the hollows which cannot, to any extent, be roughened to form a good keying surface for it to cling to. An elastic stopper which can generally be had in mahogany and teak colours, is quite good for the job, but never gets hard and is apt to contract and wrinkle slightly after some months. If it is used it will be found easier to manipulate if slightly warm ; it can be smoothed off with a putty knife moistened with turpentine and finally any excess wiped off the surface with a turpentiney cloth. A stopper specially meant for use under varnish is obtainable and is probably the most satisfactory material to use.

Two more moderately thick coats of varnish are now applied ; the first one being only lightly rubbed down. When thoroughly hard, these coats are cut well down. The surface should, after these fourth and fifth coats, be getting really smooth. If the flat of the hand is being used to press on the sandpaper when rubbing down, only the highspots and general surface of the planking will be cut down and become dulled and the hollows will remain shiny ; by wiping over the surface with a cloth and looking at it from an angle you will easily be able to tell to what extent you have achieved your object by the production of a universally smooth surface. If no shiny depressions remain, the final building up of the glossy finish may commence, but the final two coats should not be applied until the undercoat layers of varnish have been built up as a smooth base for them ; this may take as many as ten undercoats. Generally, however, a satisfactory finish can be applied over five undercoat layers and if perfection is not obtained with this number of base coats, subsequent maintenance sandpaperings and varnishings will produce the desired mirror-like surface in the course of time.

The sixth coat of varnish should be applied thinly. Its object is to fill in any slight scratches or marks of abrasion made during the rather drastic cutting down of the fourth and fifth coats. It is then lightly rubbed down with very fine sandpaper—No. 0 of the ordinary variety, or No. 400A of the waterproof type.

The hull is then dusted off with a brush. Dust is a very great menace to the final coat and even the most careful precautions are unlikely to eliminate dust specks from the finish entirely. However, every effort should be made to prevent it from settling on wet varnish. The following method is perhaps super-fussy, but it can be modified according to the time and the patience which the varnisher has and the pride which he takes in his work. First of all the floor is damped down and swept. Dust sheets or old sails are then rigged over the dinghy fairly low down, but not so low as to rub the worker's head as he varnishes; the idea of rigging the dust sheets low is to leave less room above the boat in which dust may fly about. The whole hull is then dusted over two or three times with a brush, particular attention being paid to the plank edges of clinker-built boats and the rubbing strakes, centreboard slots and around the rudder hangings of all types of hull. If the boat is on trestles, dust them off too. Next shut all the doors and windows and wait for the dust to settle down. Finally, go over the hull twice with a cotton cloth or wash leather moistened with a fifty per cent mixture of varnish and thinners ; this will pick up most of the remaining specks of dust. The surface can be gone over again a short time before varnishing, as mentioned earlier in this chapter on page 66. The final coat is then applied and should be of moderate thickness.

Here are a few DON'TS to be observed when varnishing. They apply equally to enamelling.

Don't try to varnish in wet or clammy weather. Don't varnish in cold weather if you can help it. Don't start to varnish a boat in the late afternoon—it will be cold and damp by the time you finish and all the local flies will be out for their evening constitutional. Don't try to pick suicidal insects off wet varnish ; wait till it dries and then wash them off with a wet chamois leather. Don't varnish in an open shed or out-of-doors in windy weather—flying dust, grit, pollen and leaves have no respect at all for wet varnish. Don't pour out more varnish than you can use in twenty minutes. Don't leave the job while you have lunch and expect the varnish to join up again. Don't wear a fluffy tweed coat when brushing-on and don't let any admiring friends or relations wearing fur coats bustle in to see how you are getting on. It is as well to hang a notice on the door saying " Danger ! Wild animals," " Keep out, Small pox ! " or " Caution, 20,000 volts." Don't smoke while you are applying varnish. Don't jump off the pier if you see a speck of dust on your newly varnished hull in spite of all these precautions—it is almost impossible to prevent it.

But *do* get a friend to take your dog for a very long walk for you on the day you choose to put on the final coat.

CHAPTER VII

ENAMELLING AND PAINTING

Comparison between enamel and varnish—Priming—Building up—Under-coating—Final coats—Special finishes—Hard enamels—Metallic paints—Anti-corrosive paints for metals—Metal protectives—Spraying—Polishing

THE close similarity between the composition of varnish and enamel was mentioned in Chapter IV. The application of the final enamel coat and the final varnish coat is carried out in exactly the same manner, as might be expected. The building up of the base for these final coats is, however, widely different.

The obvious difference between varnish and enamel is the opacity of the latter finish. In other words, the transparency or colour of the materials which you use to build up a smooth base beneath an enamel finish does not matter at all, whereas, in the case of varnish, a series of coats transparent throughout are required, so that the appearance of the wood may be enhanced and not hidden. It is reasonable to expect that freedom from the limiting factor of transparency enables the use of an easier and quicker method of producing a smooth surface for an enamel coat, than the more tedious method of building up with a succession of carefully rubbed-down undercoats.

The first stage in the production of an enamel finish is the sealing of the bare wood with a primer. The primer provides a sound base which adheres strongly to the wood and which, having a low permeability, to some extent prevents excessive absorption of moisture by the timber. Two coats are generally used and they can normally be applied on successive days, being allowed to dry overnight. The primer is equivalent to the first coat of thinned-down varnish applied in the case of a fully varnished finish.

It is, however, in the building up of a smooth surface that varnishing and enamelling methods differ. In the case of an enamelled or glossy paint finish, the surface should be built up by the use of a special compound which is usually applied with a broad-bladed flexible knife. The compound is generally known as trowel cement and dries hard in from four to eight hours according to the thickness of the coat. When dry, it can be sandpapered down with ease to form a firm and even base which provides an excellent keying surface for the finishing coats. There is no doubt that this material is very satisfactory and saves much time.

Two applications of undercoating should be made over the trowel cement. The object of the undercoating is merely to form a good colour base for the finishing enamel and, although many undercoatings will have fairly good filling properties, it is not desirable to use them for building up the surface. The undercoating should be suitable for use with the enamel which is to be applied and should be of the recommended shade. The best undercoatings have a high degree of opacity and therefore only thin coats are necessary. Heavy applications of undercoats should not be made, as thinner coats will be more tenacious and less liable to chip off their foundation, should they receive a blow. Undercoatings with poor properties of flow should be avoided at all costs, for some of them are inclined to brush out almost like paste and in consequence demand considerable rubbing down to remove the brush marks before any enamel can be applied ; much rubbing down should not be necessary if a smooth surface has already been built up with trowel cement and it is the height of folly to spoil such a base by using a thick covering of a poor undercoat.

A good undercoat should dry out with a matt surface which will provide a good key for the enamel, but it should nevertheless not be sufficiently absorbent to allow the enamel to soak into it at all. It should be given sufficient time to dry out properly between coats and before the final enamel is applied ; fifteen hours is generally enough.

The final enamel coat is applied in the same manner as the final coat to a varnished hull, all the anti-dust precautions being taken. Enamel also demands the same conditions of a dry and temperate atmosphere as does varnish, if it is to give the best results. Whilst the opacity of first-class enamels is very good, it is nevertheless hopeless to expect them to be completely lacking in transparency and it is scarcely necessary to mention that not only should the ground colour be correct, but it should also be clean and free from dirty fingermarks or stains.

Centreboards and rudders are probably better coated with a rather harder finish than the hull. Special enamels are made for this purpose and a very hard and smooth surface, which will give the minimum of skin friction, is produced by them. The preparation of the surface for this type of enamel is the same as for the hull enamel, but two coats of the harder enamel will generally be given instead of the single coat which should be sufficient in the case of the hull finish. Since a good thickness of enamel is built up, only one application of undercoating is really necessary and if an especially hard and tough enamel covering is required, the undercoating or trowel cement may be omitted altogether and the hard enamel applied direct over the primer. In this case the surface should be well smoothed down with fine grade sandpaper before the application of the final coat—in fact the surface is built up in precisely the same manner as in the case of varnish. After being allowed to harden thoroughly, the final coat may be cut down lightly with No. 400A W.O.D. sandpaper and burnished with a special paste and liquid-polished. Many of the common car polishes are suitable for the polishing of racing dinghy hulls, centreboards and rudders.

Personally, I should hesitate before applying the hard type of enamel finish mentioned in the foregoing paragraph to a metal centreplate or metal-bladed type of rudder. Centreplates will occasionally vibrate considerably on certain points of sailing and at certain speeds, while the metal blades of rudders are liable to twist to a considerable degree when the helm is put hard over. Such flexing of the surface would seem to call for a more flexible and less hard finish than that recommended for wooden centreboards and rudders. As an underwater covering for those boats which have to remain continuously in the water, such an enamel is excellent, for although it has no properties of antifouling, it will stand up to the frequent scrubbings to which a racing boat should be subjected, if her bottom is to be kept clean and smooth and in a state in which skin friction is reduced to a minimum.

A new type of finish, which may be used on the bottom, is technically known as a catalysed finish. It is a phenolic resin in alcohol and other solvents. An acid hardening agent is added to this syrup which is then brushed on. It dries very hard and may be rubbed down with " wet or dry " sandpaper grade 400 and burnished.

Aluminium paint is sometimes used on wooden masts, as mentioned in Chapter IV, page 48. Although few would consider a mast finished with a metallic paint so pleasant in appearance as one which is clear-varnished, there is no doubt that it makes an efficient and protective coating of very low weight. When applying finishes with metal flakes or powders suspended in them, care should be taken to stir up the paint fairly frequently to prevent the particles of metal from settling down to the bottom of the can. This is a precaution which should not be necessary in the case of normally pigmented finishes in which the pigments—and, in the case of anti-foulings, the poisons—are so finely ground into the media that very little settling down should occur.

Copper and bronze paint has also been used on spars. While this may look more attractive than aluminium, and at the same time is highly protective, it is, in fact, not wholly suitable for the task, for wherever it is rubbed by rigging and the powdered metal itself is denied the protection of its suspending medium, it will be corroded by sea water and the familiar green verdigris will be produced which will be most unsightly. Care should also be taken to keep copper or bronze finishes away from aluminium fittings, for an electrolytic action takes place between these metals and the aluminium may suffer to a considerable extent. For the same reason, aluminium paint should not be applied to copper or brass.

Aluminium alloy masts and spreaders should be properly protected from the effects of salt water by a suitable anti-corrosive primer. Usually two coats are recommended and if being applied direct to the aluminium, the metal should be properly degreased beforehand with the aid of one of the common degreasing solvents ; soap and water should not be used owing to its alkalidity, which may cause it to react chemically with the metal. It is also recommended that the surface should be slightly roughened to provide a good keying base for the primer. The roughening process will usually be carried out by rubbing over with a fine sandpaper or other abrasive, though chemical etching processes are frequently carried out commercially. Where the surface has been anodised, this is ideal for subsequent painting ; the anodised surface should not be rubbed down, for the thin protective film would be spoilt. One coat of primer on an anodised surface should be sufficient ; it cannot be too strongly stressed that this application should be made as soon as possible after anodising, for, in the first place, the surface will then be covered with minute pores which will give an excellent key (these pores subsequently close up and disappear) and secondly, the less time there is in which further greasing by handling can take place, the better.

Hollow rivets in metal masts should be sealed in some way to prevent water entering the mast should the boat capsize. This can be done by knifing a filling paste into the hole or by sticking a strip of some material over it. The filling process will usually be found more easy, but special metal foil strips are made for sealing such apertures and they have the advantage of fairing off the rivet head with the surrounding surface. These strips are coated with a thermoplastic adhesive and are applied with the aid of a hot iron. They can be painted over without any fear of the covering finish cracking.

Salt water does, of course, play havoc with most metals and while serious corrosion is generally limited to certain classes of iron and aluminium and its alloys, copper and brass also suffer to a certain extent and will quickly turn green with verdigris unless protected. There are various methods of doing this. Lanolin dissolved in cigarette-lighter fuel and brushed over the surface is one way ; the lighter fuel eventually evaporates and leaves the protecting film of lanolin adhering to the surface of the metal. A more permanent and satisfactory method is to apply a coating of clear metal lacquer to the surface with a fine brush.

Amateurs often wonder why marine finishes are not sprayed like car finishes and some imagine that spraying is a certain means of getting good results. Most emphatically, it is not. Some of the leading manufacturers even recommend brush application of their coach finishes and there seems no doubt that a more even, smooth finish can be obtained by brush than by spray. Where very quick-drying materials are used, spraying is an advantage. Though marine undercoatings may be sprayed, primers and finishing coats are always best brushed. In the case of primers, brushing works the coat well into the wood and ensures good adherence. In the case of finishing coats, a smoother " flow out " is obtained when a brush is used and there is far less danger of air getting trapped be-beneath the covering film, absorbing moisture and causing it to peel off. There is a tendency for the valleys between the globules of sprayed enamel to be bridged by succeeding globules, thereby trapping air in the " valleys."

Mention has been made earlier in this chapter of the polishing of enamelled surfaces. Varnished and metal surfaces may also be polished. Many owners of racing dinghies polish the bottoms of their hulls, also the centreboard and rudder in order to produce the highest possible gloss and thereby reduce skin friction. The practical value of this polishing is debatable and provided that the varnish or enamel is in good condition and has been carefully built-up, a slight extra gloss is unlikely to assist the boat materially to slide along in light winds. Be that as it may, few keen helmsmen will neglect to carry out any operation which may have even the remotest chance of helping his craft to the forefront of the fleet, hence the common sight of upturned hulls being vigorously polished before most of our more important dinghy races.

All sorts of queer concoctions are applied to racing dinghies in an effort to reduce their skin friction. In the days of plenty before 1939, a few people used to make up a peculiar recipe with white of egg, cream of tartar, vinegar and other ingredients. Most liquid car polishes will impart a good shine and are easy to apply. Wax polishes, if applied regularly, will build up an excellent surface which will be long-lasting and from which small scratches can be polished out ; however, heavy wax coatings are a nuisance to remove when the time comes for revarnishing or enamelling and for this reason are not recommended.

As has already been said, most dinghy owners have their particular preferences. A personal preference for the metal centreplate of my dinghy is a mixture of old-fashioned grate polish and black boot polish ! Grate polish is made of black lead or graphite. Goodness knows of what boot polish consists—it was first chosen by me because it seemed to be so remarkably tenacious when one had the misfortune to get it on one's hands. It seems to be equally tenacious on the centreplate and the two polishes—the boot polish over the grate polish—produce a shiny surface which positively defies the adhesion of water to it. It remains in that condition for a far longer time than will any other polish which I have so far tried.

It should be repeated, however, that given a proper surface in the first place, further polishing will probably do little to increase light weather ability of a sailing boat, except by boosting the morale of her helmsman and calming his pre-race nerves while he assiduously endeavours to outshine his neighbour.

CHAPTER VIII

MASTS AND SPARS

Curing twists and curves—Re-gluing—Varnishing—Spreaders—Broken halliards—Goosenecks—Flag—Mast fittings—Booms—Spinnaker booms and jib sticks

VERY often the maintenance work demanded by the actual spars of a racing dinghy is almost negligible, though the rigging requires fairly frequent attention. Chapters II and III of this book are devoted to the subject of rigging.

The spars of many dinghies are removed and kept under cover when the boat is not in use and they therefore have to stand up to very little weathering action. Even those which are not removed are not greatly effected by the weather, so long as the wood is properly protected by varnish or enamel, for rain cannot lie on their vertical surfaces for any length of time. It is, however, desirable to leave a racing dinghy in which the mast remains, turned so that the track or luff rope groove of the mast is facing away from the prevailing wind or most exposed quarter ; such a simple precaution will help to keep the wet out of the groove, which is unprotected by varnish.

Perhaps one of the trickiest jobs concerning a mast is the curing of a permanent and undesirable curve or twist in the track. Such curves may be produced as a result of the mast having been stored wrongly so that it sags unsupported in some places ; but they may also be more fundamental and due to the strong grain in the wood producing a warping tendency within the mast itself. The latter state of affairs, which may almost be compared with fifth column activity within a country as opposed to active aggression from hostile neighbours, is the more serious. There is not very much that can be done about it. Most builders, when making a dinghy's hollow wooden mast, take care to glue up the two halves so that the grain in each half is opposed to that in the other half and thereby internal stresses are balanced and the tendency towards warping is reduced or eliminated.

Warping produced from outside influences can generally be cured by simply reversing the state of affairs that brought it about. That is to say that, if a mast has been bent one way by being supported at its two ends only and allowed to sag under its own weight

at the middle, then it can probably be made to come straight by
" putting it in purgatory "—as it is sometimes called—in the
opposite direction. This is done by supporting it in the middle and
suspending weights at either end to put a counteracting bend in it.
The process is better unhurried. It is preferable to put a slight
strain on the spar for a long time, rather than a heavy strain for a
short time. Care must be taken not to overdo the cure and if a mast
is being treated thus during the winter lay-up, it should be looked
at every month or so to see what progress is being made.

Twists in the mast can
sometimes be cured by
clamping suitably shaped
wooden wedges to either side
of the mast, as in Figure 56.
By means of the leverage
afforded by these wedges,
the mast may be twisted
back to and beyond its proper
form. Twisted masts are
generally caused by intern-
ally produced stresses in the
wood and are therefore far
harder to cure permanently.

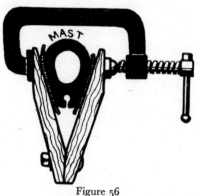

Figure 56

Small bends in a mast can often be eliminated by the adjustment
of the rigging, but it should be remembered that, if this cure is
carried out to excess, heavy unequal stresses will be set up on the
mast whilst it is in use and this is most undesirable. The logical and
proper way to cure such bends is to persuade the timber to want to
stay straight without any strain upon it. Having, by the " purgator-
ial " methods already described, got it in that happy state, the
rigging should then be used to keep it that way.

Very occasionally a hollow mast may come unstuck and the two
halves come apart slightly and show a crack between them. This
generally only occurs along the after side of the mast, as it is here
that there may be a tendency for the mast to be pulled apart by the
sideways pull of the mainsail. Masts glued up with modern casein
or gap filling adhesives should never give trouble of this nature.

Not much difficulty should be encountered in the re-gluing of such
masts and it is first necessary to force open the crack slightly with
small wedge-shaped pieces of wood. The wood forming the sides
of the crack can then be cleaned off by using sandpaper wrapped
around the blade of a knife, as in Figure 57. A gap filling adhesive
may then be applied with a thin strip of wood or a thin knife blade.
The wedges are now removed and the sides of the mast are clamped

together. The halliards should be pulled back and forth a little before the glue is set, in case any of the glue has been squeezed out of the crack and into the hollow portion of the mast wherein the halliards run ; this will ensure that the halliards are not stuck to the inside of the mast. Any surplus glue should also be cleared from the inside of the luff rope groove before it has time to set.

Masts from which the varnish has been chipped or chafed quickly go black at the bare spots, if left unprotected. It is not wise to try and scrape out these discolourations, for they may go fairly deep into the relatively soft wood and there is frequently little thickness to the walls of a hollow mast. The designer of the mast decides the minimum thickness of wood which will stand up to the strains to be imposed upon the walls of the mast and it is asking for trouble to reduce this minimum thickness of wood with a scraper. In Chapter V, page 60,

Figure 57 will be found a description of how these stains may sometimes be removed by using chemicals. It is doubtful, however, if the original clean freshness of a new mast can ever be satisfactorily restored once it has been lost and, though probably no one would dream of spoiling the beauty of a clear silver spruce mast by enamelling it in its youth, it may be found that an opaque coloured finish will improve its appearance when it has lost its original glamour.

Care should be taken when rubbing down a mast not to take too much off the corners and not enough off the flat surfaces. Three coats of varnish or a coat of primer and two of enamel are quite enough on any mast. As later coats are applied to freshen and renew the surface, an equal thickness of the old finish should be removed to give place to it. Thus the weight of an accumulation of old coats of finish is avoided. The varnish should be applied very thinly, especially to the upper part of the mast, for it is not called upon to stand up to much wear there. At the place where the clew of the foresail and its sheets rub past the mast when tacks are being changed, a rather heavy application may be made.

Aluminium spreaders should be cleaned off and protected against corrosion by aluminium paint, clear lacquer, or a thin film of lanolin. Details of such protective films may be found in Chapter VII, page 81.

The ends of spreaders should, after the diamond shrouds are fixed in them, be bound around with adhesive tape to prevent the mainsail from tearing on them. Insulating tape should not be used as it will cause black marks to be made on white sails. Sometimes foresails get caught on the ends of spreaders and this is very liable to tear the leech seam open and start to tear one of the seams between the cloths. A certain, simple, and easy way to guard against this is to bind a length of thin wire between the end of the spreader and the mainshroud, as in Figure 58. The sail positively cannot get caught on the spreader if this is done.

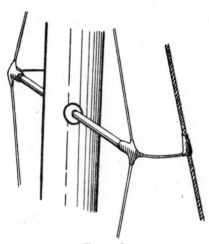

The halliard sheaves at the head and the heel of the mast should be lubricated with a little oil and halliard winches should be taken apart, cleaned and lubricated periodically. There is very little to wear out in these fittings and they are not subjected to frequent movement, but a keen eye should be kept for any signs of a weakness developing.

Figure 58

Before the two halves of a hollow mast are glued up, cords are laid in the hollow part with which to haul through the halliards after the spar is made. This cord is called a mouse ! The sparmaker makes very certain that the mouse is firmly attached to the halliard before he commences to pull it through, for if they part company in the midst of the mast, he has a nasty job on his hands getting another one through without anything to haul it with.

If either of your halliards should break, there is a way to get a new one through the mast, though it is a somewhat tricky business. A length of very light chain is made fast to a cord sufficiently long to go the length of the mast. A watch chain will do for this job— the type known, I believe, as snake chain is far the best. The mast is next stood upright by an upstairs verandah or window and the chain introduced into the mast by the upper sheave of the halliard which has parted. The chain is allowed to drop down the mast, suspended by the cord until it eventually reaches the bottom sheave. The end is then jiggled up and down until the chain is persuaded to appear through the right opening at the foot of the mast. It can sometimes be hooked out of the appropriate hole with the aid of a piece of bent wire. The halliard is then pulled through in the normal way.

Gooseneck swivel pins should be oiled frequently and the tracks of sliding goosenecks should be greased. Normally there is very little strain on a sliding gooseneck track, for the boom tends to push it in towards the mast, but when the mainsail is reefed there is a considerable twisting action on the track. The track is well suited to the resistance of this twisting because of the comparatively great distance apart of its securing screws, but should these be loosened in the slightest degree, they should immediately be replaced by a slightly stouter gauge screw before there has been any chance of the holes being enlarged and made sloppy and the mast weakened. If any of the holes have already become much enlarged, they should be plugged with a small wooden dowel glued into place ; the dowel should be of soft wood and an easy fit into the hole, for a hard wood dowel driven into the mast might easily split it.

Doctor Manfred Curry, the German scientist and small boat sailor who has probably made more investigations into the aero-dynamical aspects of sailing than has anyone else, refers to the racing flag as the " soul of the boat." Indeed it is, especially when the boat is being sailed inland (Curry did nearly all his sailing on inland lakes) where the direction of the wind is less constant than at sea. Cruising helmsmen may sometimes smile at the racing dinghy sailor's faith in his flag and may well claim to sail by the feel of the wind on his face. See Figure 59. This is all very well clear out to sea where the wind blows true and steady, but inland, amongst obstructions and on narrow waters, the wind may well be blowing in a different direction at the head of the sails from that on the water. One skilful helmsman on the Thames used to use a number of small wind indicators arranged at different heights up the rigging of his dinghy : " You pays your money and you takes your choice " was what he said. It may seem an exaggeration to some seagoing helmsmen, but it is nevertheless a fact that the author has seen a dinghy with a nice little wind *running* up through a bunch of other dinghies painfully making towards the same direction on *both tacks* against a very light air and for these latter dinghies never to feel a breath of it. The soul of a boat a racing flag may be, but in winds vertical and spiral, as well as lateral, that are encountered in some waters, it is a soul in purgatory and knows not which way to turn.

Figure 59

There are a multitude of different designs for flag fittings on racing dinghies. My own is a rather complicated one, but seems to be no better than one which I made in a few minutes to go on a borrowed boat. That which was illustrated in my book *Racing Dinghy Handling* is probably as good as any and being cheap and easy to make will be described here. The illustration in Figure 60 will make the construction of this fitting fairly clear. It will be seen that the framework to which the fabric is sewn is made of brass wire. This is bent to shape and soldered and to it are soldered brass washers which pivot on a brass round-headed screw which is fixed into the aluminium tubular mast. The weight to counterbalance the flag itself may be cast out of lead, but it can be more easily made by wrapping copper or lead wire around the frame extension

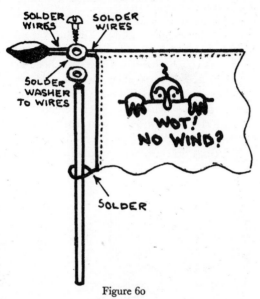

Figure 60

and smoothing it over with putty, marine glue or some other filler. Lead wire can generally be obtained from shops selling fishing tackle. The counterbalancing weight should be arranged so that it just does not completely balance the weight of the flag. The tendency for a completely balanced flag to rotate when the boat is rolling in a very little wind at sea will then be overcome. The wire frame should not completely surround the fabric, for this would make a rigid affair, which, though it would indicate the direction of the wind, would do so in so staid and dispirited a manner, that I maintain that it would be hard to place one's entire faith in it. Furthermore, the fluttering of a flag with two free edges indicates not only the direction of the wind but, to a limited extent, also its strength.

The swivelling joints of flag fittings should occasionally be oiled with a light machine oil. The fabric of the flag will need renewal fairly frequently and the seam of the foot and outer edge of the flag should be strong and adequate.

*   *   *   *   *

All the fittings fastened to the mast should be inspected frequently for security and soundness. In most well-built hollow wooden masts there will be a solid piece (except for a small hole for the halliards) at any place where fittings which have to take much strain are attached, such as by the spreaders, foresail halliard sheave, or main shrouds. Such fittings will frequently be through fastened, the rivets used being of fairly large diameter to prevent their being pulled downwards through the wood. Tubular rivets are sometimes used, for with these a large diameter rivet can be utilised without increasing the weight unduly. Emphasis is laid on the importance of fastenings of adequate diameter and the strengthening of the walls of the mast where fittings are attached, because the author once sailed in a rather gruelling race in a *Merlin 14-foot* dinghy and inspection of the rigging later showed that the mainshroud attachment, together with the upper spreaders, had been pulled down through the wood which was crushed below it to a distance of three-eighths of an inch. That occurred in two hours of racing.

If fittings do show signs of pulling downwards through the mast,

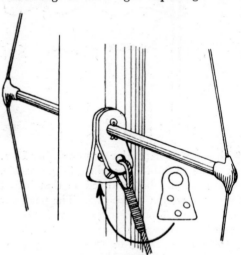

Figure 61

a metal tang may be screwed below them, as in Figure 61, to give support. But this is only a first-aid cure and a mast in which this has occurred is not really to be trusted in heavy weather. It must be remembered when screws are being put into a hollow mast, that the walls may be extremely thin ; in some cases a quarter of an inch is the thickness of a racing dinghy's mast walls. Any fastenings put into such a mast will substantially weaken it unless care is taken to place the screws so that breaking tendencies are kept to a minimum. It is dangerous to place screws so that they are directly above one another or, worse still, side by side across the grain. Figure 61, showing the tang fitted to the mast, also suggests the correct method of fastening it.

Where screwed fittings have worked loose, care should be taken

International 14-footers at Bourne End. Their sails are more easily set to perfection than those of the *National 12's* and *Merlins* which have a higher aspect ratio. The second batten of the beautifully set mainsail on *K445* appears to have become untied and will possibly be lost before the end of the race and the sail harmed.

not to replace the screws with others that are bigger than the wood can logically be expected to hold and stand. It may be necessary to plug the old screwholes and use the same sized screws again. Never use a hardwood plug or one that is oversize or else the mast may be split ; let it be an easy push fit and glue it into place.

Metal masts should not require anything much in the way of maintenance other than the possible protection of the metal with a paint of some sort. This is dealt with in Chapter VII. If any additional fittings are fixed to an aluminium alloy mast, care should be taken to see that they are of a metal which is compatible with that used for the mast, otherwise an electrolytic action may be set up between two different metals and the corrosion of one of them may be accelerated exceedingly.

Booms require attention similar to that given to masts and are likely to call for very little maintenance work. The fitting for the attachment of the kicking strap should be checked for security ; so also should the tang for the attachment of the mainsheet.

The pin for securing the tack of the mainsail in place on the boom is liable to get mislaid and it is a good plan to secure it to the boom with a short length of twine. Do not use a pin which is too long or the end of this may dig into the mast when the boat is being sailed off the wind and the boom is squared off.

If any difficulty is experienced in painting a neat black band at the sail limiting marks on the mast and boom, there is a way of making this easy. The method is simply to stick a strip of paper on either side of the place where the band is to be painted, thus masking the surface at each side. The paint can then be applied and it does not matter if it goes over the inner edge of the paper a little. The paper is soaked off after the paint is dry. Figure 62 will explain this simple dodge.

Spinnaker booms and jib sticks are generally of a very simple pattern with a hook at either end for the attachment to the clew of the sail and to the mast. Frequently the inner end of the boom

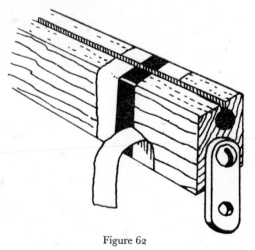

Figure 62

hooks into an eye, or small metal bracket with a hole in it, fixed to the mast at about the height of the gooseneck, or perhaps a little higher in some dinghies. The outer hook on the boom or jib stick goes into the clew eye of the sail or into the eyesplice or tuck in the sheet itself. Such a spinnaker boom has the advantage of being similar at both ends and this possibly eliminates a certain amount of confusion when the thing is being put into operation.

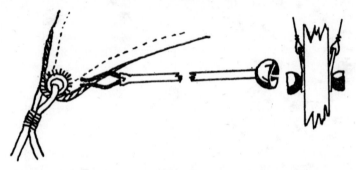

Figure 63

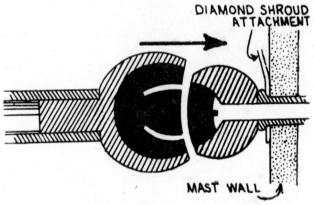

Figure 64

In the case of jib sticks, however, such fittings are rather unsuitable, for there is no need for the fittings at either end to resist an outward pull. The tendency is for the sail to push the jib stick towards the mast—not to pull it away. A hook is therefore clumsy and inefficient. Figure 63, which is reproduced from *Racing Dinghy Handling*, illustrates a jib stick which I devised for my dinghy and which has been found very satisfactory. The inner end simply consists of a cup or socket which is shaped as shown in Figure 64.

Four saw cuts are made in the sides of the cup and this allows the sides to spring outwards when it is pushed on to the ball fitting on the mast, afterwards firmly gripping the mast fitting, though allowing a wide degree of rotation in all directions. The outer end merely consists of a spring prong (formed of two small pieces of diamond shroud rigging wire). When this prong is pushed into the clew eye of the sail, it stays there by virtue of the spring action. There is no doubt at all that this type of fitting is easier to use than most and even cold and fumbling fingers will not be foiled by it.

Rigging screws need frequent lubrication with grease. The heavier the grease, the better, as it will stay on the job. A little of the grease should be smeared over the threads of the rigging screw ends, but it is preferable to do the serious lubrication by pushing grease into the ends of the body, so that, when the screw is inserted and turned up, the ends will drive the grease down the threads.

If rigging screws are wired up after the correct adjustment of the rigging has been made, and they are not unscrewed when the mast is removed, it is a wise plan to smear grease around the neck of the screw and push a little into the hole in the body into which the spike goes when adjustments are being made ; finally, the whole rigging screw may be bound around with adhesive tape to keep it waterproof.

When masts are removed by unscrewing the rigging screws, it is preferable to leave the body on the end of the screw to which the rigging is made fast. This will prevent grit from getting on the thread of the screw should the shrouds drop to the ground when the mast is unstepped or carried to its store.

It is always advisable to wire up rigging screws when trailing a dinghy, for they have a most uncanny way of being unscrewed by the vibrations of trailing and the bodies are liable to get lost. The same applies to the thumbscrews screwing the gliding goosenecks in position in some National 12's Rockets and Merlins.

CHAPTER IX

BLOCKS, FITTINGS AND FASTENINGS

Purchases—Plastic blocks—Winches—Fairleads—Rudder Hangings—Keel bands — Slot flaps — Toestraps — Floorboards — Buoyancy apparatus — Screwing—Nailing

BLOCKS and fittings should be given a look over once every few weeks. At the end of the season, or at least once a year, they should, as far as is practical, be dismantled, cleaned, lubricated and reassembled.

There can be no denying that, providing sufficient attention is given to lubrication and maintenance, the common clothes-line pulley block at sixpence a time may give quite satisfactory service as a mainsheet block on a dinghy. With a rigid maximum price rule, down to which many builders find it difficult to make a dinghy, it is only to be expected that it is on such things as blocks that economies are made in order to keep the prime cost of *National 12's* and *Merlin* dinghies within the rules. Many dinghies in these classes have collected much-coveted trophies when using blocks which could be purchased for a few pence at any ironmongers.

The value of easy-running blocks, however, should not be underestimated, especially when sailing off the wind in light fluky weather when the sheets should be trimmed to meet small shifts in wind direction. At such times, poorly moving blocks may be an absolute curse.

Nowadays it is only very seldom that blocks with wooden cheeks are seen on racing dinghies. It is also most uncommon to see modern racing dinghies with the mainsheet led to the helmsman's hand from a block on the boom ; in nearly every case the sheet leads from a block on the transom or horse of the boat. The usual arrangement of mainsheet for dinghies with more than one hundred square feet of sail is shown in Figure 65, while that for boats with less than one hundred square feet is shown in Figure 66. Perhaps it is as well to point out that while adequate purchase is desirable to reduce the strength required to handle the sheet when the dinghy is close-hauled in a blow, the increased power gained by added purchase means that more sheet has to be handled to trim the sheet a given amount ; so that, when turning from a run on to a beat, it is almost impossible to get the sheet in quickly enough if

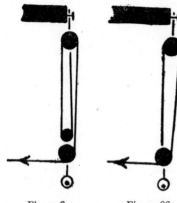

Figure 65   Figure 66

there is more than a single purchase, for a racing dinghy spins round so rapidly. In other words, what is gained in power by increased purchase has to be paid for by added lengths of rope to handle and increased frictional resistance. It is necessary therefore to strike a happy medium and to realise that what is gained on the swings is lost on the roundabouts ; it has to be decided whether the swings or the roundabouts are the more important. In light airs it may be thought desirable to reduce the purchase to less than that normally used.

The more expensive double blocks are usually of a pattern known as fiddle blocks. They owe their name to the form in which this type of block was usually made in the days of square-rigged sailing vessels, though they have little resemblance to a violin today. See Figure 67. Such blocks are more efficient than ordinary double blocks in which the sheaves are side by side, because the various parts of the tackle are kept clear of one another and there is no friction between them. Until recently most *International 14-footers* used blocks of aluminium alloy which were light and fairly resistant to corrosion. If lubricated well, these blocks were quite satisfactory. In other dinghy classes the better types of blocks used were generally made of gunmetal, but were similar in other respects to the ordinary galvanised iron pattern which plays so important a part in the support of the nation's laundry lines. More recently, blocks have been made with stainless steel cheeks and brass or gun-metal pins and sheaves.

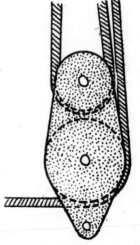

Figure 67

The latest types of blocks are made of bakelised fabric or some other form of plastic. There is no doubt at all that these plastic blocks are far superior in every way to metal ones and anyone who has had a long experience of them will be satisfied that this is so and that they run more easily than any others. I have used a pair of such blocks since 1939, and have never had to do anything to them. The cheeks are usually made of sheet material and the sheaves turned out of the same type of bakelised fabric or paper. This material is very strong in compression or tension, though it is not so well able to withstand heavy strains in shear. The sheave, which should not be bushed, usually runs on a brass pin. The beauty of plastic for this job is that it is quite unaffected by sea water and in fact the material has the property of being water lubricated ; further, plastic materials may be had with a certain amount of graphite filler compounded in them and such materials are self-lubricating.

The pins of normal metal blocks may have to be knocked out at the end of the season so that the sheave may be cleaned up and corrosion removed. However, this should not generally be necessary and instead the blocks may be rinsed around in tepid fresh water to dissolve any salt adhering to them. They may then be dried (by popping them into the oven after it has been vacated by the family dinner and is cooling down with the door open) and thoroughly lubricated. The secret of well-running metal blocks is frequent attention with the oil can ; a light type of bicycle oil is best, as heavier oils tend to make the sheave stick slightly to the cheeks. Little and often is the principle to be followed in the lubrication of blocks and sheaves.

Salt is, of course, the greatest opponent of smooth-running gear on a boat and although fresh water definitely causes swifter deterioration to varnish than does salt, the freshwater sailor is more than compensated by the fact that his gear should be relatively free from corrosion. Even stainless steel is not entirely proof against corrosion in salt water, though it may be almost negligible, and the surest way of keeping metal gear in proper running order is to rinse it frequently with fresh water and protect it with lubricant. Non-moving parts may be coated with lanolin or clear lacquer as described in Chapter VII, page 81.

Halliard and centreboard winches should seldom need attention apart from fairly frequent lubrication. Mast screw-jacks should also be lubricated fairly frequently.

Jib sheet fairleads of the deadeye type should require nothing to be done to them. A little linseed oil on lignum vitae or hardwood deadeyes improves their appearance slightly but possibly softens them as well and so they are probably best left alone. Polish and varnish both tend to make the sheets cling slightly when hauled tight and there will be less friction if the wood is left undressed. Sometimes the wood of the deadeyes will shrink and the securing strap will become loosened ; the bolts should then be tightened to keep the deadeye firmly in place, for a loose one is liable to be split and a split one may nip the sheet and cause it to jam.

All fittings screwed to the hull should be tried to see if they are quite secure. If they are loose do not merely drive the old screws in again, for if they have loosened once they will do so again. New screws should be used and they should be longer or of stouter gauge. If the wood does not permit the use of a larger screw, the fitting should be moved slightly so that the screws can bite into new, firm wood. In some cases, when a longer screw cannot be used, it may not be possible to move the fitting from its original position; in this case the hole should be plugged with a softwood dowel glued into place with a waterproof adhesive; the same sized screws should then be driven into this dowel.

The fastenings on rudder hangings are rather liable to work loose, especially if the rudder has at any time gone aground. The

Figure 68

lower pintle is frequently arranged as in Figure 68, in which it will be seen that the fitting forms the after end of the keel band and is screwed up into the keel. Good long screws can generally be used here, as they can be driven up into the stern knee which is usually bracing the transom to the keelson or hog. The upper gudgeon—and sometimes the lower pintle—is generally through-fastened to the transom. Occasionally such fittings are merely screwed to the transom and it would seem that this is not a very desirable method of fixing; flat-headed countersunk bolts are better and should be secured by means of nuts over large washers, which will spread the pressure and strain over a larger area of the wood. If the fittings have one fastening above the other, as in Figure 69, these fastenings will be made through the transom and into the stern knee; it is possible to use long screws in this position and these should prove adequate for the job. In the author's opinion it is preferable to have

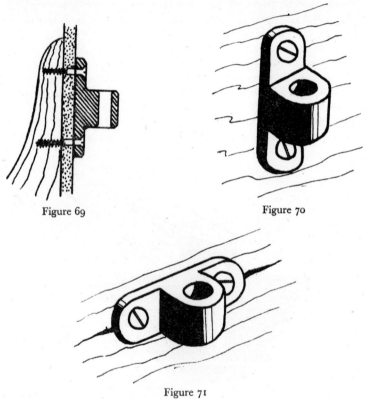

Figure 69

Figure 70

Figure 71

the fastenings one above the other, as in this way any tendency towards the splitting of the transom may be reduced; see Figure 70. Figure 71 shows how fastenings side by side may cause the wood to split.

Keel bands may get a lot of wear if the boat has to be launched by sliding down a concrete slipway. Brass or gun-metal bands will usually stand only about three years of this harsh treatment. Galvanised steel bands are sometimes used and they do stand up to scraping much better than brass, but the zinc coating is soon worn off and the steel is then exposed to corrosion and rusts. In fresh water it is doubtful whether the little rust which is formed will reduce the life of a keel band of steel to that normally enjoyed by a brass one, for the rust is doubtless rubbed off every time the boat is launched and so the keel band is kept bright—if not smooth. In salt water the accelerated rusting of the steel would probably reduce the life of such a keel band to less than that of a brass one.

Owing to the rocker or curve of the keel of a modern sailing dinghy, only a small portion of the keel band will get much wear. The part worn will probably be on either side of the centreboard slot. This is fortunate, for, as the rubber flaps which are usually fitted along the slot have to be renewed fairly frequently and to do this the covering keel band has to be removed, the two jobs can often be done at the same time and a new keel band fitted when the slot rubber is being replaced.

Although a few dinghies have their keel bands made in one length from stem to stern, most of them are divided as in Figure 72.

Figure 72

It will be seen that the removal of the portion of the keel band which gets worn—that on either side of the centreboard slot—does not interfere with the wider bands at either end, which should seldom, if ever, require to be renewed. This is a good thing, for the portions of the keel band at either end are, in the best built boats usually shaped to fit the keel accurately and are therefore more difficult and expensive to replace. Suitable material for the keel bands by the centreboard slot can be easily obtained and requires no shaping. Some owners prefer to use a half-round section material, but my personal choice is a flat section with rounded upper corners, for it is my contention that, having a wider bearing surface, it wears better ; flat sectioned material also fairs smoothly with the portions at either end. This type of section is shown in Figure 76, and is a standard material.

If the keel band has become much worn the securing screws may have had their heads cut down and it may not be possible to remove them with a screwdriver. If the head is not too much reduced, the slot for the screwdriver may sometimes be deepened by cutting it with a cold chisel and hammer. On the other hand, if the head is made so thin that it is not possible to cut an adequate slot, the only thing to do is to cut the band, prise it up and bend it back as shown in Figure 73. It will then break off on either side of the hole for the next fastening ; see Figure 74. The next portion can then be prised

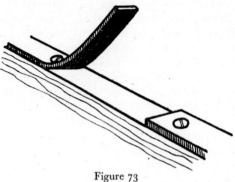

Figure 73

up and broken off. The screws can later be withdrawn by turning them with pliers.

In order to avoid the recurrence of such difficulties with worn screws it is a sound policy to countersink the screwheads in the new keel band well below the level of the surface, as shown in Figure 75. A suitable filler can then be knifed into the depression remaining above the screwhead and the surface levelled off. Alternatively, soft solder may be run into the hollows and no difficulty should be encountered in chipping this out when the screws have to be removed again later on. It will be realised that no filler can be expected to stand up

Figure 74

to the dragging of the boat on her keel band and it will probably be torn from the screwholes fairly frequently ; but it is a simple matter to knife some fresh filler into place before any important races.

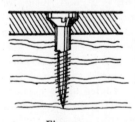

Figure 75

There is no doubt that rubber strips at the bottom of the centerboard case serve three very useful purposes. Firstly and most important, they reduce drag due to eddying and disturbance in the centreboard case. Secondly, they prevent water splashing up out of the centreboard case and into the boat. And thirdly, if they are fitted really well, they enable a completely waterlogged boat to be bailed, even though the top of the centreboard case may be below the level of the water, so long as the bailer can beat any waves slopping in over the gunwales.

The rubber is rather liable to get torn and must generally be replaced fairly frequently. Plain rubber strip is the best stuff to use and rubber " insertion " (one or more layers of fabric sandwiched between rubber) should be avoided because the fabric is liable to shrink when wet and this will cause kinks and deep wrinkles on the surface like corrugated paper. If the rubber has to be cut, use a sharp knife and lubricate it by rubbing a well-licked finger over each side of the blade ; ordinary water will lubricate a knife which is cutting rubber, but there is nothing better than honest to goodness spit. The rubber should be stretched out slightly and tacked into position with copper tacks. The edges of the two strips should be touching, or should overlap slightly. The keel bands should then be fitted and screwed down over the rubber wich will then be firmly clamped in place.

One of the chief causes of the rubber getting torn and worn is the fact that, when the centreboard is raised, the rubber gets nipped up into the case and against the sharp edge of the keel as shown in Figure 76. The remedy for this nipping of the rubber is simply to radius off the centreboard slot as in Figure 77. It is a pity that this

Figure 76   Figure 77

is not done when the boat is built, but it only takes a few moments to do and is very well worth while. Of course, if the radiusing is done, the bare wood should be painted or protected by some preservative coating before the rubber is replaced.

The old strip rubber from the centreboard case slot may be utilised to prolong the life of toestraps. Dinghy toestraps have an important function to perform and must be maintained in a fit condition to carry out their job. It is rather remarkable that toestrap breakages should be as frequent as they are, for the cost of replacement is so slight and the effects of their carrying away is usually undignified, to say the least of it. It is perhaps acting the spoil-sport to endeavour to reform dinghy owners in this respect, for there is no doubt that to see the helmsman and crew straining out in a tough blow, then their feet flying upwards, while with a simultaneous splash they do a backward somersault, is a sight worth seeing.

Toestraps are usually made of canvas and are screwed to either end of the centreboard case and clamped up underneath the centre-thwart as in Figure 78. If the straps are merely screwed to the centre-board case, it is strongly recommended that the plate method of fixing be substituted, as the plate, if screwed up tightly, will spread the strain on the canvas and lengthen its life. This is where the strip rubber discarded from the centreboard case slot comes in for further use, for it can be utilised with advantage between the metal clamping pieces and the canvas, also between the canvas and the centreboard case or centrethwart. Figure 79 shows how the rubber is used

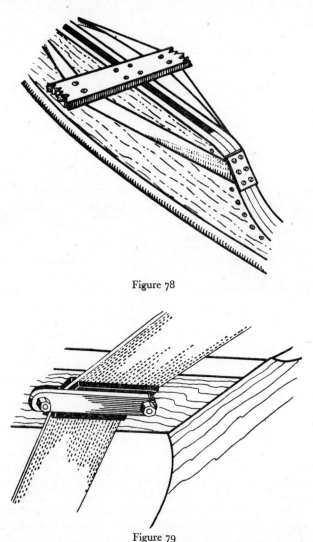

Figure 78

Figure 79

in the case of the centrethwart clamp. If this method is adopted and good quality canvas webbing is used, toestraps should give faithful and reliable service for a number of years. Their life may be further prolonged by using a canvas preservative on them and now and again rinsing any salt out of them.

Floorboards are another item upon which the equilibrium of the crew may depend. Slippery floorboards are a menace both to performance and comfort. While the tendency to slip may be much reduced by slatted or bare wood floorboards, they can be made even safer with a little care.

There are two alternative methods of making floorboards more or less skid-proof, both of which are neat and long-lasting. The first is to cover them with canvas, which can be turned up underneath the slats and tacked in place as shown in Figure 80. The second, perhaps better, way is to give them a surface like fine sandpaper, which will afford an excellent foothold. The floorboards must of course first be removed from the boat. The top surface of the slats is then covered with a medium thick coat of varnish ; this is a good way of using up an old can of varnish that has got a little lumpy or bitty.

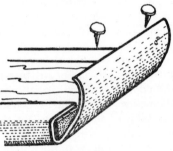

Figure 80

The varnish is allowed to get tacky and then fine dry sand is liberally sprinkled over it. It is not important to spread it absolutely evenly, but it should cover all the new varnish. After allowing an hour or

Figure 81

so for further drying, the slats are up-ended and tapped on the floor several times, as in Figure 81, to dislodge the excess sand. They should then be allowed to dry thoroughly, when a light brushing over with a dusting brush will remove any other particles of sand which are not very securely anchored. A coat of thinned-down varnish may then be applied over the sand and this will flow around the particles and firmly bed them in position. The appearance of floorboards treated in this way is not unpleasing and, when clean, the grain of the wood may be seen through the sand, if the latter is of a fine clean quality. If the job is done properly this finish should last a very long time ; the floorboards of one of my dinghies show no sign of wear after nine years. Considered logically, this is understandable, for it is the method that is adopted in the re-metalling of roads—with tar instead of varnish, and stone chips instead of sand—and it is the sand itself that is taking the wear and not the varnish.

* * * * *

Buoyancy tanks and bags should be carefully inspected and any leaks attended to. Rubber buoyancy bags can, of course, be repaired with a bicycle tyre repair patch and the instructions for doing this simple job are always given with the repair outfit. It is wise to look over the buoyancy bags for any signs of chafe or contact with sharp objects and to stick a patch on these places whether there is a leak or not. The cause of any leaks should also be sought and if it is due to a fixture in permanent contact with the surface of the bag it should be covered with a little adhesive tape to render it less damaging.

The bolt through the centreboard case on which the centreboard pivots should occasionally be removed and inspected for wear. This should not be necessary more than once in three seasons. Care should be taken, when replacing the bolt, not to overtighten it or the sides of the centreboard case may be pulled together slightly and strained, with consequent leakage.

All attachments to the hull for standing and running rigging, such as the stemhead fitting, shroud plates, mainsheet horse, centreboard tackle plates and so on, should be checked for security and the fastenings renewed if necessary.

Perhaps it would be helpful to mention a few hints on driving screws. Brass screws are fairly easily broken if they are being driven into hard wood and care should be taken not to use too much force upon them. If two pieces of wood are being screwed together—for example, a wooden cleat to the centreboard case—the upper piece should be drilled so that the screw is a push fit into it ; the screw should not have to be driven into it nor should it be a sloppy fit. This hole should then be countersunk if flat-headed screws are being used. A smaller hole should be then made in the lower piece of wood so that it is slightly shallower than the depth to which the screw will be driven and of rather less diameter than the shank of the screw—disregarding the thread. Figure 82 represents the four stages in the procedure of fixing by screws.

The holding action of the screw depends on the spiral cutting thread

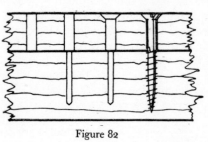

Figure 82

and the head ; as the screw is driven into the wood, the thread bites into the timber of the lower piece and the head draws the parts together. Unless the holes, illustrated in Figure 82, are provided for the screw, the thread will not function properly and the holding power will be reduced ; in hardwoods there will be a danger of the head being broken off or the slot being damaged. When driving screws into hardwoods it is always advisable to lubricate them with something ; a little candlegrease rubbed on the thread is excellent. Avoid screwing into the end grain of wood whenever possible, as the screw threads will sever the fibres of the timber and the holding power will be much reduced. It is sometimes advisable, if a brass screw has to be driven into very hard wood, first to cut a bed for it with a steel screw of similar size.

Copper nails demand a certain amount of skill when being driven into hard woods. Though it is, of course, unusual to drill a hole for an ordinary iron nail, it is the general practice where copper nails are being used. The diameter of the hole should be about three-quarters of the breadth of the nail. This will be sufficiently large to permit the driving of the nail without it bending and will ensure that sufficient side pressure on the nail is exerted by the surrounding timber to enable it to maintain a firm hold. Generally speaking, nails are not used in boatbuilding where there is likely to be much parting strain on the joined members and screws would generally be used in such a situation.

Where " through-fastening " is possible with copper nails, they will either be bent over and clenched, or riveted over rooves. The overlapping parts of the planking of clinker-built boats are usually secured together by means of copper nails cut off and riveted over rooves, which are dome-shaped washers which are a driving fit on to the nails. In most racing dinghies the ribs are fastened to the planking by driving the nails through the planking and ribs and clenching over on the inside. The skins of double and treble-skinned carvel-built dinghies are fastened together in the same way.

Rooves are put on to nails by means of a rooving punch, which is a heavy punch with a hole up the centre in which the nail fits as in Figure 83a. The nail is then nipped off about $\frac{1}{16}$ in. from the roove (83b). A heavy hammer or iron weight is then held against the nail head on the outside and the cut end is tapped over the roove with a light ball-headed riveting hammer (83c). A well-riveted nail should be drawn up tightly in this manner and it is a bad practice and an indication of poor workmanship if nails are " hardened-up " by giving them a direct and heavy blow with the flat face of the hammer, for it results in the nail being bent in the wood with consequent weakening of the latter and general reduction in the efficiency of the fastening. Figure 84 shows a nail to which this has been done.

Nails which are clenched are generally cut off at an angle about $\frac{1}{4}$ in. from the surface of the wood as in Figure 85a. The head of the

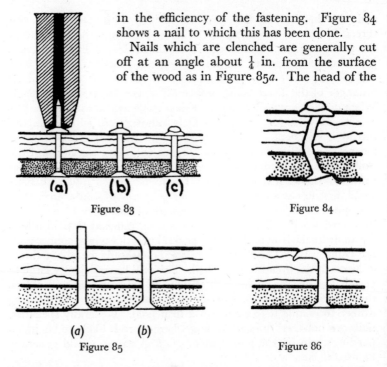

Figure 83

Figure 84

Figure 85

Figure 86

nail is then held up with a heavy hammer or weight and its cut-off point given a blow with another hammer. This first blow of the hammer will bend the tip of the nail over to form a hook, seen in Figure 85b. The nail is then gently tapped in the direction of the grain of the wood and will eventually lie flush with the surface with its hooked end firmly grasping the wood, as shown in Figure 86.

Sound gear is called upon to play its part in moments like this. A fouled foresail sheet is almost capsizing one of the *National 12's*, whilst all the others are sailing with the modicum of uncertainty usually associated with a heavy-weather gybe.

CHAPTER X

CENTREBOARDS AND RUDDERS

Smoothing centreplates—Straightening bent plates—Metal toes—Centreboard pivots—Buffers—Rudder shapes—Rudder sections—Drop rudders—Rudder heads—Tillers—Joysticks

THE surface and shape of centreboards and rudders is of the utmost importance. It is not part of the task of a book on maintenance to discuss the merits or demerits of various shapes of these fittings, but it may be pointed out that the keen dinghy owner can do a great deal towards the improvement of the performance of his boat by careful attention to them. Rudders are not difficult to make, nor are wooden centreboards, and experiments with different shapes are extremely interesting and may be advantageous.

The treatment of the surface of wooden centreboards and rudders has been dealt with in Chapter VII and the only recapitulation necessary here is to emphasise that these two together comprise a very large proportion of the entire wetted surface of the dinghy and every attention should therefore be paid towards getting a smooth and slippery surface.

Certain classes of dinghy are not permitted to use wooden centreboards and are restricted to the use of mild steel centreplates. It is not so easy to obtain a really smooth and lasting surface on these as it is on a wooden board because, although a good layer of enamel may be built up to cover any unevenness of the metal, this is rather liable to chip and flake off when undergoing the harsh treatment to which it will probably be subjected.

Perhaps one of the best methods of obtaining a lasting smooth finish on a steel plate is first to get it heavily galvanised. Unfortunately this deposit of zinc is liable to be more or less uneven and the resulting surface may be very far from that desired ; modern methods of galvanising may improve the finish obtainable. Provided that the steel plate was smooth in the first place (apart from the usual pits and general roughness) the zinc can be scraped down until it is perfectly smooth, without any fear of leaving the steel unprotected, if the following method is adopted. The galvanised plate is covered with a thin coat of an elastic type of enamel—one which will not easily chip. The entire plate is then scraped with a metal scraper ; this tool is pushed, not pulled as in the case of the paint

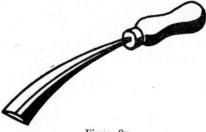

Figure 87

scrapers mentioned in an earlier chapter. Figure 87 shows the type of tool used. In this way the high spots of the zinc deposit will be removed and the whole surface levelled. So long as some of the enamel remains in the hollows one is assured that a film of zinc remains to protect the steel underneath. The scraped zinc finish will be almost as smooth and as shiny as a chromium finish. Great care must be taken not to remove too much zinc where the edges of the plate are bevelled. When the scraping of the plate is completed it may be polished with a metal polish and then protected with a wax polish of some sort. A satisfactory mixture of polishes is mentioned in Chapter VII, page 82.

Occasionally centreplates may get bent, especially in these days when most owners and designers are anxious to get plates which are as light as possible and therefore made of thin gauge metal. It is not usually difficult to straighten a bent plate, but great care should be taken not to overbend it in the other direction, for frequent bending back and forth will greatly weaken the material. Probably the easiest and best way to straighten a plate is to put it between two rigid members and exert pressure on it as shown in Figure 88. An iron grating will do to provide the resistance against which the plate is bent and, since these are present as rain water drain coverings in almost every road, the difficulty of finding one is not great, though one may feel a little self-conscious about manipulating a centreplate under the public gaze in a well-peopled thoroughfare.

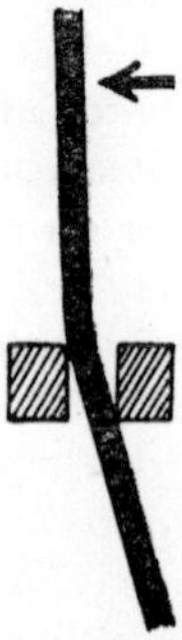

It takes a hard knock to nick the toe of a metal centreplate, but every now and then it becomes necessary to remove such nicks. Sometimes a certain amount of good can be done by tapping with a hammer, but generally the only cure is to file off the projecting

Figure 88

bits. This, of course, will remove the protective zinc and the spot should be touched up with a little anti-corrosive paint and polished. It may be sufficient, if the boat is only sailed on fresh water, simply to polish over the place with a good wax polish.

The lead toes of ballasted wooden centreboards are far more susceptible to nicks than are other types of centreboard toes. They should always be protected as much as possible by a hard metal capping along the edges and over the tip, but even with such protection the lead will suffer knocks every now and again and, being so soft, may have fairly deep pits gauged in its surface. Unevenness can usually be remedied to a large extent by the intelligent use of a light hammer, the metal being tapped back into place. On no account should an attempt be made by an unskilled metal worker to apply heat to the lead in order to soften it and allow it to run back into place. When the lead is back in place it may be smoothed off with a file and sandpaper and finally varnished or enamelled.

The leading edge of any wooden centreboard should always be protected by a metal band screwed to the wood.

The wood of a centreboard should not be called upon to act as the bearing surface for the pivot. Frequently a metal plate is screwed to either side of the wood and these plates bear on the centreboard pivot pin ; but this is not a very well-designed arrangement either, for the metal-to-metal bearing surfaces are very narrow and excessive wear is caused to the pin at either side as in Figure 89. A more suitable bearing for the board is shown in Figure 90 and it will be

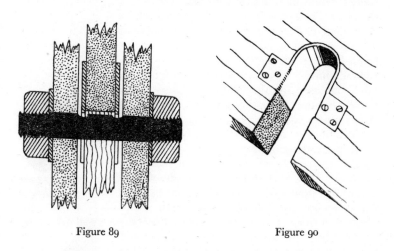

Figure 89   Figure 90

seen that this is an arrangement that anyone handy with tools can make and fit in half an hour and for a few pence.

Some form of buffer should be fitted to the uppermost arm of the centreboard—that to which the tackle is attached. This will prevent the board or plate from doing damage to the centreboard case or centrethwart if the tackle runs out with a rush. Instances have been known when the shackle attaching the tackle to the plate was pulled down between the sides of a plate case by a runaway centreplate and jammed there securely, so that all efforts to raise the plate were of no avail while the boat was still afloat.

Two ordinary rubber door stops can be used to make an efficient buffer and these can be had very cheaply in almost any iron-monger's shop. Figure 91 shows how these are as-sembled to form the buffer, so that, even should the tackle break, the falling plate cannot do much harm to the boat.

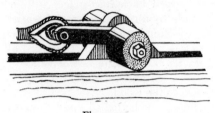

Figure 91

Rudders are inclined to get chipped on their leading edges almost as much as centreboards and should also be protect-ed by a metal strip.

Many helmsmen have a variety of different rudders for different conditions. For instance, a deep narrow rudder, such as in Figure 92, may be found most efficient at sea, but such a rudder would be a liability on the tideway of the river Thames, where there is frequently a great deal of flotsam having a nasty habit of getting caught up on the centreboard or rudder. When racing at such a place as this, a rudder similar to that shown in Figure 93 might be used, as this would be more likely to remain free from flotsam and the leading edge is not so liable to get chipped.

Figure 92

Some builders of boats do not go to the trouble of properly shaping the section of the rudder. While the profile of the blade is more or less important, the sectional shape is of vital importance and no racing dinghy owner can afford to have a rudder blade which is not properly formed in section. Luckily the mat-ter is generally fairly easy to remedy and merely involves the cutting away of undesired wood, but if the blade has been made too thin it will not be possible to do this to a sufficient extent to produce the proper form. The blatantly wrong section of blade, which is generally produced for reasons of economy rather than from ignorance, can be seen in

Figure 93

Figure 94. It will be noted that the edges have simply been radiused to a small degree. Unfortunately economy is not the only factor in

the production of wrongly sectioned blades and one not infrequently sees it recommended that blades of a streamlined form should be used, the particular shape advised being similar to that shown in Figure 95. Now while this section may be perfectly correct for something travelling through a compressible medium such as the air, it does not necessarily follow that it will be correct for something travelling through

Figures 94, 95 and 96

a much denser and incompessible medium such as water. It would seem that the more correct shape would be as in Figure 96. The thickness of the sections is exaggerated for the sake of clarity. Anyone who can spare the time to fix a rudder in a stream of water in which particles of some solid are suspended can see for himself the action of these two types of section. Such an experiment is often very simple and merely consists of anchoring a dinghy in a stream of muddy water—below a weir or by a floodwater outlet into a river—and peering over the transom into the water. The solid particles will show the course of the water stream over the blade of the rudder and the eddies created may be studied.

When embarking on the job of cutting down the edges of the blade it is generally wise first to strip off the varnish or enamel, as this may blunt the planes and spokeshaves which you will use for fairing the wood. The shape of the section can be checked by holding a straight edge across it. The maximum thickness of the blade should be about one-third of the way from the leading edge.

Of course the metal blades of dropping rudders cannot be made to the correct section, for they are too thin. One wonders if they could with advantage be fattened up by fastening wooden cheeks to the metal with some wood-to-metal adhesive.

Many expert helmsmen do not like to use drop rudders if they can avoid doing so, because the blades are inclined to be a bit " sloppy " between the cheeks of the rudder, with the result that a direct and certain contact with the blade cannot be felt through the helm. No one of experience in dinghy racing will deny the importance of proper direct and rigid contact between the rudder blade and the tiller and any suggestion of backlash may be most disconcerting in fluky winds when immediate response to the slightest touch on the helm is essential. For this reason it is most important that the tiller should be a proper fit in the rudder head. Sloppiness of the tiller in the rudder head is an extremely common fault in dinghies and one which the simplest cure is liable to have undesirable effects.

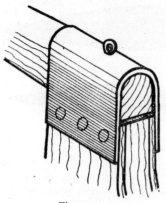

Figure 97

Most tillers are held in the rudder head by a pin, as shown in Figure 97. This is a simple and satisfactory method up to a point— that point being when the tiller shrinks or is compressed by the pressure upon it. The answer to that situation may appear to be easy enough and it may be thought sufficient either to pad out the tiller a little, with shavings glued to it, or else simply to tap the tiller further in to the rudder head and drill a new hole for the pin so that it is kept in that position. But there is a snag to this remedy in that,

should the dinghy capsize and the tiller remain immersed for a little time, the wood of the tiller will swell and become so tight a fit in the rudder head that it may become impossible to remove it by normal

means, so that considerable difficulty may be experienced when bringing the boat ashore. However, the safest method is probably also the easiest ; it is merely to immerse the tiller end in water every now and again, so that it will be kept a good fit.

For those who dislike the crudity of a simple pin to hold the tiller in position the following idea may have some appeal. Being somewhat addicted to gadgets and complications myself, I feel that it should be said that there is no virtue in a complicated method of doing something, unless it does its job better than a simple method ; simplicity may often be the key to efficiency. The following idea guarantees having the tiller held firmly in place in the rudder head.

Figure 98

116

To make the tiller safe against swelling and jamming during cap-
sizes, the tiller end should be painted thoroughly ; then thin copper
or brass sheet metal should be tacked over the surfaces which are in
contact with the rudder, so that the paint is protected and not worn
off as the tiller is slipped in and out of position. The gadget in
question is best explained by means of a diagram and is shown in
Figure 98. It consists of a thumb-screw affair so shaped that the
mainsheet cannot get caught on it. This thumb-screw engages with
a threaded brass tube in the end of the tiller and this is held in position and against rotation by a brass facing-piece to which it is brazed
or soldered. No further explanation is needed.

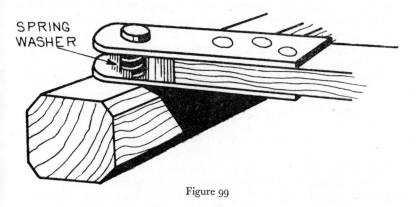

SPRING
WASHER

Figure 99

Tiller extensions or joysticks are a standard fitting in all modern
racing dinghies. Being rather thin as a rule, they are fairly susceptible to breakage, especially at the point where the pin goes through
for attachment to the tiller. The hole for the passage of the pin
considerably weakens the wood at this point and, as there is a
tendency for some helmsmen to pull upwards on the extension and
so bend it by the pin, it is here that they generally snap. The arrangement shown in Figure 99 greatly increases the serviceability of the
tiller extension and will allow of a certain amount of upward movement without in any way straining the wood. As will be seen in the
sketch, two thin strips of metal—brass or, preferably, stainless steel—
are riveted on either side of the extension. These strips are held
apart by a spring washer through which goes the pin of the tiller.
There is an ordinary flat washer at either end of the pin and between the tiller and the bottom metal strip of the extension. The
pin is riveted over at either end. The rigidity of the extension on
the tiller can be increased, if desired, by simply tightening up the
rivet by tapping its head up with a ball-headed hammer.

CHAPTER XI

SAILS 1—GETTING THEM RIGHT

Stretching new mainsails—Stretching new foresails—Correct sheeting of foresails—Flow—Importance of straight luffs—Foresail hanks—Tension on halliards and outhauls—Leech lines—Battens—Tying a reef—Roller reefing

No boat can sail well without good sails, any more than a car can run well without a good engine. Bad sails lose dinghies more races than do ill-kept hulls or inefficient gear. Like elephants, sails never seem to forget and a few hours of harsh treatment or neglect may be held up against you for the rest of their life, whilst they tease you with irremovable creases and wrinkles and hold you at the tail of the fleet.

New sails demand special care during their first few hours of life. This applies particularly to mainsails. Dinghy mainsails are usually made of Egyptian cotton which is particularly closely woven. The closeness of the weave is more important from considerations of reducing friction rather than permeability, which is so slight that it can be ignored (it has been shown that permeability reduces the drive of a sail by only 0.6 per cent when the boat is close-hauled). The bolt ropes which are sewn to the luff and foot of the sail are made of Italian hemp. Now both of these materials—the cotton cloth and the hemp rope—are liable to stretch and shrinkage, and both will absorb moisture ; but the yachtsman's worry is that they do not stretch and shrink to the same degree, neither do they absorb moisture at the same rate. This unequal reaction of the materials of the sails to conditions of moisture and tension is one of our biggest troubles when dealing with them.

When a new sail is made, the sailmaker allows for the greater stretch of the bolt rope by stretching it out fairly taut when sewing the cloth to it. The result of this is that when you receive the sail it will have small crinkles along both the luff and the foot, due to the cloth being puckered as the artificially stretched bolt ropes are relieved of the tension put upon them by the sailmaker—in fact, as a racing sail, it will look deplorable. If the sailmaker has done his job skilfully, however, proper and patient handling on the part of the owner is all that is needed to produce a well-setting sail. New sails should never be used for racing straight away, but should first be set on a dry sunny day when there is a light breeze.

The mainsail should be hauled out along the boom so that the wrinkles along the foot just disappear. The outhaul should be made fast when this tension is reached. The battens will of course be inserted before the sail is hoisted and the leech line—if any—should be left absolutely slack. The sail should then be hoisted so that the wrinkles are just eliminated from the luff, when it will be stretched out to the " made length." The made length is the size of the sail as made by the sailmaker and before the canvas is sewn to the bolt ropes—the size of the fabric itself, in its new and unstretched condition.

Although the deep wrinkles may have largely disappeared from the luff and the foot, the sail will have quite a lot more stretching to do and its appearance will still be very creased. Most well-known firms of sailmakers use a staggered stitch these days when sewing the cloth, as this type of stitch is supposed to facilitate the more even stretching of the fabric along the seams. There are, however, some excellent sails still made with straight stitch sewing and I think it fair to say that I have seen very bad and very good sails made by either method.

When you leave the shore with your new sails set, cruise around for a couple of hours, never really going very close-hauled or trimming the sails hard in or else you will put undue strain on the leech, which will stretch more quickly than the rest of the sail. It will be found that the luff and the foot will become slack as the sail stretches and this slack should be taken up by the halliard or downhaul for the luff, and the outhaul for the foot ; but there is no need to sweat up or haul taut on either of them. Just let them stretch naturally under the effect of wind pressure and do not attempt to force the pace, or you may stretch one part more quickly than another, with the result that the weave of the cloth is pulled out of shape and lasting damage done. After two hours the sails should begin to appear smoother and more shapely and it is permissible to use them for racing after this length of time, though three or four hours of such tender treatment will be even more to their advantage. If the mainsail has not stretched out to its marks on the boom by the time the minimum stretching period of two hours has expired, it is not a matter for great concern, for it will probably stretch a good deal more under the weight of a heavier wind and rather harsher treatment of the sheets, halliards and outhauls, which it will get when being used for racing.

Foresails do not need such careful attention as mainsails, because they have a wire luff-rope to which the canvas is sewn and it is intended that there shall be no stretch in this part of the sail. The luff may therefore be set up as taut as usual the first time the sail is set. Nevertheless the canvas of the sail has to stretch and it is most certainly advisable that this stretching is done slowly and carefully by the light pressure of a gentle breeze, and the influence of the sun.

A badly setting foresail is a double menace in that it will almost certainly upset the efficiency of the mainsail as well as failing to do its own job properly. It is probably true to say that more foresails are spoilt by the incorrect lead of the foresheets than from any other cause. Modern foresails are made so that their cloths form a mitre seam running from the clew to the luff and roughly bisecting the angle at the clew. The correct angle for the sheet of a foresail which is being used with a Bermuda mainsail, in which little twist is allowed to develop at the head, is as in Figure 100. It will be seen in this figure that the sheet is pulling slightly downwards from the mitre line. The effect of this downwards pull is to eliminate excessive twist and sagging off to leeward at the head of the sail and to allow a little more flow or belly near the luff. If the best results are to be obtained from your sails, however, this must not be accepted as a hard and fast rule, for a mainsail which is allowed to twist considerably when being used, either on or off the wind, should be in company with a foresail in which there is also considerable twist ; otherwise the upper part of the latter sail will backwind the mainsail luff about half-way up.

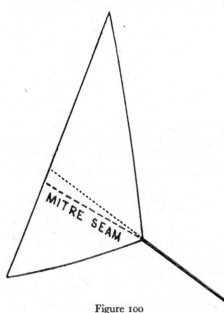

Figure 100

Only experience can determine the precise and ideal position of the fairlead from the observation of the behaviour of the luffs of the mainsail and foresail when close-hauled. A foresail luff which has too much flow, produced by a fairlead placed too far forward, will have the appearance of being starved of wind when closehauled ; whilst the effect on the mainsail, of a foresail so sheeted, will be to backwind its luff from one-third to two-thirds of the way up. A sail so sheeted may also develop a curl inward at the leech ; this is a very serious condition, as it will create eddies and upset the smooth flow of air on the leeward side of the mainsail.

It should be borne in mind that it is impossible to beat to windward properly with a foresail that is too full at the luff, although it has been shown that the luffs of sails do at times actually operate efficiently with a negative angle of opposition to the wind of as much as sixteen degrees and care should be taken not to flatten the sail too much. It should, however, also be remembered that the mainsails of many dinghies—especially *International 14's*—are cut very full and have a great deal of flow in their forward part, which is frequently unavoidably backwinded by the foresail in spite of the correct sheeting and trimming of both sails. Too much twist in the foresail, caused by a fairlead placed too far aft, will manifest itself by a fluttering of the leech of the sail towards the head. This will be more noticeable in stronger winds when, even if it cannot be seen, it can often be heard.

The flow or belly in a sail is produced by the skilful making of the sail and is of great importance from considerations of aerodynamics. Most dinghy sailors are well aware of the importance of the correct arching of the sails and are familiar with the fact that more driving power is produced as a result of negative pressure, or suction, on the leeward side of the mainsail, than is produced by positive pressure on the windward side. The reason for the importance of the arching of the sail to produce belly or flow is that the shape of the sail then *bends* the current of air from its normal path without tearing jagged eddies from it. Figure 101 will help to explain this and represents the approximate windstream on a dinghy mainsail.

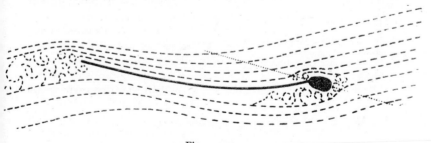

Figure 101

It would seem logical to believe that the correct angle of incidence for the luff of the sail to make with the windstream is about nought degrees. This means that, allowing for the apparent wind effects caused by forward motion, the angle of the fore and aft line of the boat with the luff of the sail should be about twenty-seven degrees.

(The majority of racing dinghies sail at an angle of about forty-five degrees to the real wind, thus making tacks of a little less than ninety degrees to one another. A dinghy tacking thus at four knots in a six knot wind will be using an apparent wind of twenty-seven degrees on her bow.) If it be granted that these conclusions are reasonable, and given a properly cut mainsail, how can we ensure that the luff of the sail does, in fact, present the correct angle of incidence to the windstream? The answer lies in the straightness of the luffs of the sails.

Flow is put into the sails by cutting them so that the luff and, in the case of sails set on a boom, the foot have a convex curve on their edges. This is shown in the much exaggerated diagram in Figure 102, in which it will readily be seen that when the luff and foot are pulled out straight along the spars, there will be a slackness in the canvas which will assume a belly or curve under the effect of wind pressure. The important thing to remember, therefore, is that sails cut with the proper amount of curve must be set on straight spars to produce the correct flow. Furthermore, it is of little use to have a spar that is straight when the sail is not working, but which bends immediately there is any strain upon it. It is truly amazing to see from photographs the degree of bend that is present in the masts of many dinghies on the wind. If one bothers to take a look up the mast of a dinghy when beating—sighting along it as along the barrel of a rifle—one is likely to be still more surprised. It is stressed that this should be done on the wind, not because the mast bends more on this point of sailing than any other, but that the elimination of bend in it is far more important when close-hauled than when running. Jumper stays and forestays can generally be made to effect a cure.

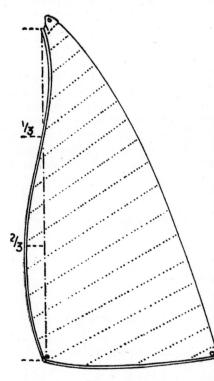

Figure 102

The same rule applies to foresails—their luffs should be kept straight. Since the luff of a foresail depends solely on tension for its support, it is hardly necessary to state that it should be hoisted as taut as is practical, due consideration being paid to the strength of the halliard and the luff rope of the sail.

In many *National 12-footers*, *Merlins* and *Fireflies* the luff of the foresail is hanked to the halliard itself, so that any tendency to sag away to leeward when under way is reduced by half, for the halliard is automatically sweated-up tight by the sail. Figure 103 shows this type of arrangement, which, though very satisfactory from most points of view, has certain disadvantages which render it far from ideal. It is not a method of rigging which can be utilised in dinghies which may wish to lower their foresails when under way—for instance, when running with a spinnaker—because, owing to the impossibility of passing

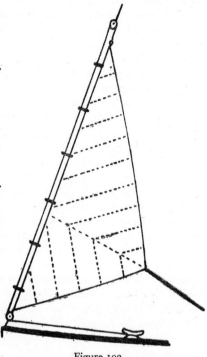

Figure 103

the rope tail of the halliard through the foresail hanks, one is unable to get the sail down when afloat ; such an arrangement can scarcely be considered seamanlike.

Another method of getting a taut forsail luff is to set the halliard up with a small lever, or a rack, as in Figures 104 and 105. A little rigging screw may be incorporated in the lever arrangement and the halliard adjusted to precisely the correct tension by this. A fourth method of ensuring a straight luff is by means of halliard

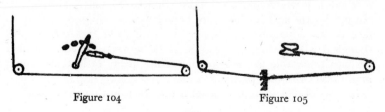

Figure 104   Figure 105

winches, as found in the *International 14's* and other classes which are permitted to use them. By means of a winch, or the lever just described, the halliard may be adjusted to exactly the right tension. The ideal tension would seem to be a little greater than that on the forestay when the dinghy is sailing closehauled in a light air ; this will mean that the first strain will come on the halliard, and the forestay will only take the strain when the halliard has stretched a little and the weight is more than either it or the foresail luff should be expected to stand. It should be remembered that the foresail halliard, being longer and of relatively lighter and more flexible wire rope, will stretch considerably more than the forestay.

The foresail hanks which are in common use on ninety per cent of racing dinghies are excessively clumsy and heavy, whilst instead of the foresail receiving an almost completely smooth flow of wind, the air is torn on these oddly-shaped contraptions. No doubt there are many who will disagree with the contention that foresail hanks are of very little value, if any, and that the disadvantages of their disturbing effects on the windstream outweigh any slight assistance which they may render towards maintaining a straight luff to the sail. If the sail is hoisted to the right tension, as directed in the preceding paragraph, there is little support needed from the forestay, although the foresail halliard will undoubtedly stretch in a strong breeze. It is quite true that the luff of an unhanked foresail will be seen to sag away considerably from the forestay, but on the other hand if, in a boat whose foresail is made fast to the stay, a cord is rigged from the top splice of the forestay and is made fast taut to the lower forestay attachment on the boat, it will be observed that the foresail, and the forestay to which it is hanked, sag off to a degree that is not perceptibly less than that to which an unhanked foresail will. A certain amount of " sweating up " effect on the forestay must take place by the action of a sagging foresail hanked to it, and by this means the stretch in the stay will partly be taken up earlier, but the difference which this makes is probably so slight that it can be ignored. These remarks apply more especially to foresails of relatively small area with a high ratio of length of luff to foot— such as the sails seen in the *National 12's*, *Merlins* and *Fireflies*. On boats which are rigged somewhat haphazardly by hit and miss methods and which may have rope halliards, or no method by which tension on the foresail luff may be accurately adjusted, it may in fact be an advantage to support the sail from the forestay, for though it will tend to sag away in loops between the hanks, this is perhaps preferable to the excessive falling away to leeward which might otherwise take place.

By way of defending this belief it may be said that the foresail of a *National 12-foot* dinghy has been used for a number of years both hanked and unhanked and, though conclusions are very hard to arrive at when considering the effects of small changes in the rigging of a dinghy, there can be little doubt that the performance of this boat is, in fact, better to windward when hanks are dispensed with.

If hanks are to be used, then let them at least be light and create as little obstruction to the wind as possible. Those shown in Figure 106 can be made out of stiff wire (diamond shroud piano wire will do) for a few pence and in a few minutes. To remove them, they are simply given half a turn and the forestay can slide out from between the two curved arms of the hank.

Figure 106

The tension on mainsail halliards and outhauls is of relatively less importance, but most assuredly no racing dinghy helmsman can afford to ignore the demands of these for sympathetic adjustment. The mast and boom of racing dinghies are generally provided with black bands beyond which the mainsail must not be hauled out, but this is not to say that the corners of the sails should never venture away from these marks. The black bands are the limits to which the sail may be pulled and are fixed so that at no time is too much sail area gained by allowing the sail to stretch after it has been measured. When the sail is at the marks it should be at the maximum stretch to which it is ever likely to be subjected ; if the sail stretches beyond the black bands, it may have to be cut down a little or the black bands moved and the entire sail plan altered accordingly. The sail will by no means always be pulled out to its maximum stretch and should reach the black bands only on dry, windy days, when the fabric of the sail can be expected to stretch to its utmost and any reduction in flow, which a heavily-tensioned luff and foot might produce, would be an advantage and would counteract the bagging or bellying effect caused by heavy wind pressure. On damp days, or when the wind is light, the sail should be hauled out less far, and least of all when wet weather is associated with little wind.

Once again, experience and common sense are the best guides. Let us, for instance, take the case of a sail which has to be used on a damp day on which it is not actually raining and there is a moderate breeze ; the sail will probably have absorbed a fair amount of moisture, even though stowed in a canvas bag, and this will have caused the canvas and bolt ropes to shrink a little. Now since the bolt ropes probably run in grooves in the mast and boom, they are unable to dry out at all, but the sail on the other hand has a stream of air passing over it and may dry a little and stretch naturally. The luff and bolt ropes should therefore be pulled out fairly taut, so that they may be artificially stretched to the same degree as that which the canvas may be expected to reach. This will require a greater tension on the halliard and downhaul than would be required on a drier day. If, on the other hand, it is a day on which the rain is actually falling, the sails will get wetter and shrink more than the bolt ropes, which are protected from the wet in the grooves in which they run ; on such a day the bolt ropes should be left slacker. It is as well to remember that even if the sails are not in use, the bolt ropes will absorb more moisture on a damp day and shrink more than the canvas of the sails which is sewn to them. No hard and fast rules can be made and there are no definite guides, other than the good judgment and consideration of the conditions under which the sail is called upon to work. Neither the tension on the bolt ropes nor the distance of the corners of the sail from the black bands can be taken as guides by themselves, but both should be taken into account when the sail is hoisted.

Leech lines, which are cords running in the seam of the leech of the sails, are to be found in most racing dinghy mainsails and in a number of foresails. Generally speaking, they are best left alone and quite slack. Their object is to increase the fullness or flow in the after part of the sail, but they tend to produce a curve in the leech similar to that shown in Figure 107, especially in foresails, which have no battens to help them resist this curling. A word may be spoken

CURL IN LEECH

Figure 107

in favour of leech lines when considering their presence in the foresails of *International 14-footers* and other dinghies with large overlapping foresails which are inclined to foul the spreaders ; they will keep the leech of the sail intact, even if several of the seams have been torn by spreaders and the sail will continue to draw after a fashion instead of blowing about like a hoist of signal flags. Figure 108 illustrates this point.

If a leech line is used and allowed to have sufficient tension on it to influence the set of the sail, remember that, like the bolt ropes, it too will absorb more moisture from the atmosphere on a damp day than will the fabric of the sail and will, in consequence, shrink more. A leech line in use should never be tied out to the end of the boom so that it cannot be undone with ease while afloat, but should be made fast to a small cleat from which it can be eased without any difficulty.

Two dinghy sailors deep in thought over their *International 14's*. Perhaps the owner in the foreground is wondering how he can reach up to fix the binding which is coming adrift from the end of his lower spreader.

Figure 108

Sails which are provided with pockets should never be set without battens. The consequence of using a sail without battens is to stretch the canvas between the head and the clew in a straight line and cause folds which may persist throughout the life of the sail. Most dinghy mainsails are cut with an outward or convex curve in the leech, so forming an area of sail between the leech itself and an imaginary line joining the head of the sail to the clew ; this area is termed the roach and is unmeasured and gratuitous sail area in most classes. The task of sail battens is to hold the roach and the after part of the sail flat, thereby spreading the strain uniformly across it. The battens should be about half an inch shorter than the pockets, so that the inboard end of the batten pocket is not worn or chafed by the pressure of the batten upon it.

As was mentioned before, Bermuda mainsails are meant to be set with their luffs held straight. Bends in the mast will naturally affect the set of the sail ; but perhaps it will be even more adversely affected if the tack of the sail is held in a boom which is too far from the mast to permit the luff to assume a straight line throughout its length and which pulls the lower part of the luff sharply aft from

H   129

the mast groove or from the lower mast slide. The main offenders in causing this undesirable state of affairs are bulky gooseneck fittings.

*　　*　　*　　*　　*

Most racing dinghies are provided with roller reefing, but there are a few which tie down reef points and earings when reducing the area of sails. Amongst the latter are *Cadets*. The correct reefing of such sails is most important, for a badly reefed sail may be spoilt very easily and all too frequently does one see the operation carried out wrongly on all classes of vessels. Once again common sense should indicate the correct way and a little reflection on the matter will quickly show that there is a certain obvious procedure to be followed.

When tying down a reef in a dinghy, the sail should usually be lowered before the operation is commenced, because otherwise the boat may become unmanageable while the job is being done ; if the task is to be done in a sheltered spot alongside a quay or even ashore, a neater reef can probably be accomplished if the sail is up. Let us consider the latter case : first of all the weight of the boom should obviously not be supported by one small point on the sail, wherever it may be, and the spar should therefore be lifted either by hand or by a topping lift ; it is not very likely, however, that a topping lift will be fitted to most small dinghies. If the reef has to be taken in single-handed, it will not be possible to take the weight of the boom all the time and, that being so, the sail should first be lowered until the large eyelet on the luff of the sail, opposite the line of reef points to be used, is just above the top of the boom. It should then be secured in this position by passing a line—or earing, as it is called—through the eyelet or reef cringle, under the boom, and so on until it is made fast. Any strain which may have been placed on the sail while the luff earing is tied, will have been taken by the luff, which is roped and therefore able to withstand it without any ill-effects ; but the boom should now be lifted up and supported on your shoulder whilst the leech earing is used to tie down a similar reef cringle on the leech of the sail, which, not being strengthened by a bolt rope, must not be allowed to run the risk of stretch which the weight of the boom would impose upon it. The foot of the sail should be stretched fairly taut along the boom when the leech earing is tied. The sail may now be rolled up neatly and the two outer sets of reef points—nearest the clew—tied under the foot bolt rope of the sail. The reef points should *not* be tied under the boom, for such a reef will not be so tidy and the bolt rope is the part of the sail which is designed to take the strain of the foot—whether direct or through reef points. There will probably be six or seven reef points in line on the average dinghy mainsail and after tying the outer two or three—using your shoulder to support the boom all the time while doing this—it will be safe to allow the sail to take the weight of the boom, for the strain will now be spread over a fairly wide area. The two inner sets of reef points—towards the luff—may now be tied and finally those in the centre, commencing at that nearest the clew which is still left untied. When all the points have been tied, the main halliard should be hauled upon to tighten the luff, and the topping lift, if any, should be slacked away. In unreefing, the reverse of the above process is carried out. If this simple method is followed, no harm will come to the sails.

Roller reefing is simple enough and the only precaution to take is to see that the sail is rolled up evenly and that the leech is pulled out towards the end of the boom.

Sails should never be left reefed on the boom, whether rolled or tied.

CHAPTER XII

SAILS II—KEEPING THEM RIGHT

Resetting stretched sails—Battens—Reefing—Damp and rot—Rinsing—Drying—Folding—Stowing—Nylon—Washing sails—Removing stains—Smoothing—Repairs and patches—Reef points—Wire luff ropes—Nylon spinnakers

IN spite of the best of good intentions towards his sails, the racing man may at times have to abuse them, even though he may be aware of the fact that he is risking the set of his canvas. For if a boat is being raced seriously, she will at times be treated brutally and demands made upon her which would, or should, never be made upon a hack boat ; though the care lavished upon her when she is not racing will possibly be tender to the point of seeming ludicrously pernickety to those of the salt-encrusted, dyed-in-the-wool, cruising fraternity.

Apart from repairs and normal maintenance work which will be necessary from time to time, it may also be advantageous to mention that sails which have been pulled out of shape may sometimes be made to set perfectly again by various methods. Furthermore, badly made sails can sometimes be pulled into shape. Methods somewhat reminiscent of those in vogue at the time of the Spanish Inquisition are used, the rack being a strong favourite. One would hesitate to recommend the novice to attempt any such operations without the practical guidance of one more experienced, but nevertheless sensible and thoughtful treatment can sometimes make silk purses out of sows' ears.

For instance, let us take a mainsail which had to be reefed right down in a blow, so that the bottom batten had to be removed because the pocket was rolled around the boom ; later in the race the wind dropped and the reef was shaken out, but it was impossible to insert the batten again in its pocket. The result of this was a sail of which the leech was stretched unevenly, causing heavy folds to run down the after part of the sail to the clew, as in Figure 109, in which the creases are caused by tension in the direction of the folds.

The cure for this state of affairs might lie in the following procedure. The area affected should be thoroughly wetted, so as to cause shrinkage of the fibres, for the folds arise from the fact that the fibres running down parallel to the leech—at right angles to the cloths of the sail—have been stretched, while those running in the direction of the cloths have not. The weave of the fabric has therefore been pulled out of shape as in Figure 110, which is enlarged and

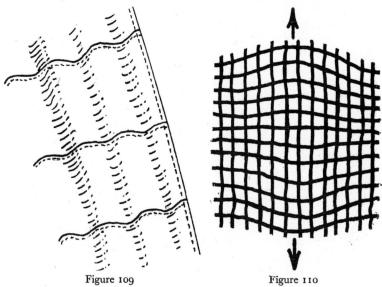

Figure 109   Figure 110

exaggerated for the sake of clarity. The sail is then held in such a way that considerable tension can be put on it along the direction of the affected cloths, as is shown in Figure 111. It is allowed to dry while under this tension. The effect of this should be to pull the weave back into shape. The area treated in this way may be found to have been stretched more than the rest of the sail and a bagginess may result. This can be cured by soaking the whole sail in fresh water and drying it carefully, suspending it every two feet by its luff from a taut line ; subsequently the sail should

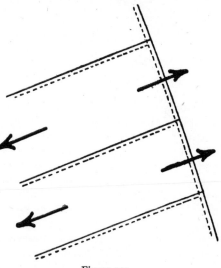

Figure 111

be stretched in the same manner as a new sail, though the stretching period may be much shorter.

A common tendency in dinghy foresails is the development of a fold or crease a few inches in from the leech. This was mentioned in Chapter XI, page 126. It is very hard to cure this fault and I venture to say that the only really effective remedy for this very serious condition is to cut off that part of the sail which is curling over. This is a case where the leech line might have prevented the curve developing, by taking the downwards pull instead of letting it be borne by the fabric of the leech of the sail ; but this would probably have thrown too much belly in the after part of the sail and upset its efficiency accordingly.

Another common fault is a ridge or crease running along the inboard ends of the batten pockets as in Figure 112. The causes of

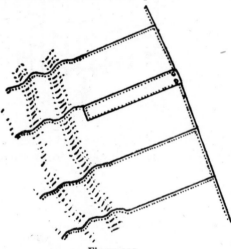

Figure 112

this may be twofold. Firstly the roach may be too great to be supported by the rest of the sail in spite of the battens. Secondly the battens may be too stiff at their inboard end and be unable to bend to the general curvature of the sail. In the latter case it is very easy to thin the battens down a little towards their inboard ends. Sometimes such a crease may be produced by leaving battens in a sail which is not in use ; battens should always be removed from a sail when it is not being used.

Battens themselves demand and deserve a little careful attention. Their object, as has been mentioned before, is to extend the roach and leech of the sail and ensure that the whole of this area takes an equal strain. In performing this task they should interfere with the natural curve of the sail as little as possible. We previously went into the question of the arching of the sails and it was pointed out that the greatest curve, or flow, in the mainsail was in the forward part and that it should flatten out progressively towards the leech. In order that this type of curve may be encouraged rather than hindered, the battens should be made so that they will assume the correct curve for the area of the sail in which they are positioned ; each batten may have to be made differently in order that this aim may be attained and should be numbered or named so that it can always be used in the right place.

The upper batten extends almost right across the sail, whereas the lower batten only extends about one-third of the way across—in the leech area, where the sail is relatively flat. This surely draws one to the logical conclusion that the top batten, which has to assume the sharper curve towards the leech, should be more flexible than the lower one. Furthermore, since the inboard end of each batten will be expected to follow the sharper curve towards the forward edge of the sail, it follows logically that this end of the battens should be more flexible than the outer end which will have to assume a flatter curve. This difference in flexibility throughout the length of the batten will be more marked in the upper battens than in the lower ones. It should also be pointed out that the battens used in light weather may be too flexible to be suitable for use in heavy weather ; a variety of battens should be kept and care exercised in the selection of the correct one for the conditions prevailing.

A number of different materials are used for battens, wood still being the most common, though various types of plastics, such as perspex and bakelised papers and fabrics, have more recently been seen. If wood is used it should be of a type suitable for the job ; ash is probably the best, though beech and birch are also commonly used—oak and mahogany will stain white sails when wet and should therefore be avoided. Wooden battens should be given a thin coat of varnish or aluminium paint to prevent excessive absorption of moisture in wet weather.

The varying flexibility throughout the length of the battens may be achieved in a number of simple ways, the most obvious and best being the tapering of the material towards the inboard end. It can also be done by gluing or riveting thin veneers or sheets of the material on either side of the outboard end of the batten. Again, it may be accomplished by cutting away an area down the centre of the batten to a varying degree or even by drilling an increasing number of small holes towards the inboard end. The latter three methods are shown in Figure 113. The last two methods are

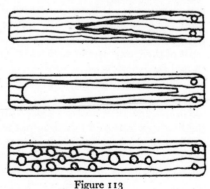

Figure 113

not to be recommended as the batten will have to be of a uniform thickness and, if thick enough to be sufficiently stiff at the outboard end, the tension and compression strains on the faces at the inboard, and more bent, end will be proportionately far greater than they would be in the case of a batten tapered down to a thin section ; they would therefore be more liable to break. It should perhaps be mentioned that a batten which is too flexible may do as much harm to the set of the sail as one which is too stiff. Battens should always be stowed on a dry, flat surface so that there will be no tendency in them to warp out of shape.

When a sail is roller-reefed, it may be something of a problem to know when sufficient sail has been rolled down to warrant the removal of the bottom batten. It is probably fairly safe to say that the batten will do very little harm, if any, to the sail, even if it is kept in place until its tip reaches the boom. It is almost certainly better to retain it, than to take it out and find later that you are forced to increase your sail area in a lightening wind and have to use the full mainsail without the bottom batten.

*   *   *   *   *

The greatest enemy of the sails themselves is damp. Most dinghy sails are removed from the boat when she is not in use ; but even so, unless proper precautions are taken—especially when the boat is used at sea—there is a great danger of dampness affecting the canvas. It is common knowledge that salt has an affinity for moisture and, if sails which have been splashed with salt spray are simply dried and stowed away, they will, however carefully kept in canvas bags, absorb moisture from the air in damp weather and become little short of saturated, whereupon they will become liable to the evil effects of mildew and sail rot. Every time a sail gets salt spray on it, therefore, it should be rinsed off in fresh water and allowed to dry thoroughly. It is not necessary to soak the whole sail, but only those parts which are actually salty ; and it is seldom necessary to do the bolt ropes as well, for these are frequently protected from most of the spray by the grooves in which they run. Little difficulty should be experienced in washing off the salt from the cloth without actually soaking the bolt ropes, which would subsequently take an inconveniently long time to dry. Of course, if the foot bolt rope is salt-impregnated from heavy spray dripping down the sail and into the foot rope groove in the boom, then it too will have to be rinsed.

The best way of rinsing salt from sails is to lay them flat on a lawn, or on concrete or cool tarmac (beware of hot tarmac, for the molten tar may stick to your sails) and hose them down, or swill them over with a few buckets of fresh water. They should then be turned over and done on the other side. Bits of grass and grit may get stuck to the wet surface of the canvas and look very messy, but they will shake off as the sail dries and, providing the washing is done on a reasonably suitable site, the sails should not get dirtied.

It frequently happens that a race finishes with a run off the wind and under these conditions the sails, which may have been spattered by spray when going to windward, dry off before the end of the race, so that on reaching the shore they may not at first sight appear to have been wetted. On close inspection little circles of crystallised salt may be seen on the canvas, but if the sail has been allowed to shake, most of this more obvious salt may have been flicked off ; in the latter case the best way to find out if there is in fact salt on the sails is to taste them. There is no need to lick the entire suit of sails—the foot of the foresail and the tack of the mainsail are the most likely spots to be affected !

When drying sails (and sails which have been splashed with fresh water will, of course, also have to be dried before being folded and stowed away) they are probably best suspended by their luffs from a taut line to which they should be fastened every couple of feet, so as to keep the luff straight. Sometimes sails may be seen suspended by their heads from the signal halliards on the yard-arms of club ensign staffs, but although the luff then hangs down vertically in the position in which it is when on a dinghy, the sail is then inclined to flap about excessively and it is doubtful if it is really good for it. One thing is quite certain and that is that it is a very bad practice to hang wet sails so that their surfaces lie parallel to the ground, for the weight of the wet canvas in this horizontal plane will most likely pull great bags and bellies in the sail. Sails which have been rinsed should of course be allowed to stretch gradually for a little while before being subjected to rigorous racing conditions.

The sails having been rinsed and dried should then be carefully folded and stowed in canvas bags in a dry place. There are many ways of folding sails and some are no doubt better than others ; the following method seems to keep sails in good setting condition and is fairly easy. The mainsail is at first folded in half, parallel to the leech ; then in half again in the same direction. The now narrow folded sail is folded over and over at every foot or so of its length until eventually it forms a flattened roll, similar to a swiss roll which has suffered from being in the bottom of someone's

Figure 114

shopping bag when several pounds of potatoes have been emptied on its squashy torso. Figure 114 will help to indicate what is meant. The virtue of this method is that the first folds go at right angles to the cloths and so these and subsequent folds are made in the direction of the threads in the weave. Various stages in this method are shown in Figure 115.

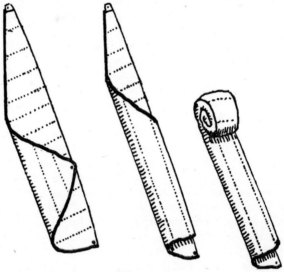

Figure 115

The principle underlying the method of folding the foresail has the same object in view as in the plan which has just been described for folding the mainsail. The first fold brings the clew of the sail to the point on the luff where the mitre seam strikes it. In other words, the mitre seam is folded back on itself. Another fold is made parallel to the first, again folding the sail in half. Finally the luff wire is carefully coiled from the head to the tack—and the sail is rolled with it. See Figure 116. The rolling or coiling of the wire luff-rope is important so that kinks and sharp bends may be avoided. The sails may then be stopped up and slipped into the sail bag.

Foresail sheets should always be coiled down and left outside the sail bag, as they are apt to retain a lot of moisture which might damp the sails. The neck of the sail bag should be tied up firmly to keep out the damp atmosphere and it may be mentioned here that, at any time when the canvas boat cover is being waterproofed (see Chapter I, page 12), it will do no harm to treat the sail bag in a similar manner. It is wise to turn the sail bag inside out every now and again to let it dry in the sun and to kill off the spores of the fungus which causes sail rot.

Nylon spinnakers are not easily affected by rot and, being used only before the wind, such care is not needed in the folding of them, for a few creases in them do not matter.

Most of us like to see white sails that are clean and are conscious of our " I-thought-my-spinnaker-was-white-until-I-raced-against-Sir-Jasper " attitude towards them. Most sailmakers will undertake to clean sails and this they do by scrubbing them with soap and water : of course they know best, but it always seems rather drastic treatment and liable to chafe and roughen the surface of light canvas.

If it is decided to attempt the washing of sails at home, they should first be soaked in lukewarm water. A lukewarm soapy mixture can then be mixed up in the bath (a little household ammonia added to the water will be found a helpful ally in the battle against dirt) and the sails put into this and pummelled up and down so that the soap suds are squeezed through the fabric. Personally, in order to carry out the pummelling process efficiently without breaking my back, I remove my shoes and socks, roll up my trousers Blackpool-Bank-Holiday fashion, then, standing in the bath, perform a sort of ritual dance on the sails. I may mention that this process was not quite so happy in the old days when my dinghy mainsail had angular metal slides sewn to the luff ; in those days the dance was liable to be punctuated by wild and anguished cries. When the water shows signs of suspending most of the dirt that was in the sails, the plug is withdrawn and the dirty water committed to the care of the local district council. It is better not to attempt to take the sails out of the bath before rinsing, as the resulting drippage on the floor is unlikely to prove popular. At least four rinsings should be given to make sure of getting all the soap out and the sails may then be hung up to dry

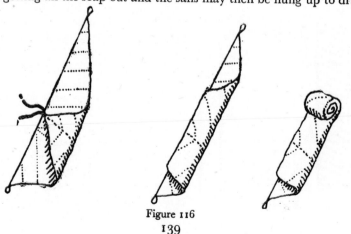

Figure 116

as previously described. They should not be twisted or wrung out, as this is liable to spoil the shape.

Dirty sails have been sent to the laundry and the results have proved less ruinous than might at first be expected. I was once astonished to see a laundry label at the tack of a friend's sails and was told that it was his regular practice to have them laundered every year. It must be, however, a somewhat hazardous business and an action which one would not initiate without serious qualms.

Rust stains on white sails may be removed with a warm solution of oxalic acid. One ounce of the oxalic acid crystals should be dissolved in one pint of warm water. The sails must be rinsed thoroughly after this treatment, but if the rinsing is properly carried out they will not be harmed.

Generally the drying of newly washed sails will complete their treatment, but for those who are super-fussy one thing yet remains to be done. It has been demonstrated that the surface friction on the duck of racing sails can be reduced by as much as forty-five per cent by sticking down the fibres hanging from its surface with a coat of varnish, whilst it is reduced by forty per cent if the projecting fibres are singed off with a flame. Whether this friction has any appreciable retarding effect on the forward motion of the sails against the windstream is doubtful, but there can be little doubt that this friction does cause turbulence along the surface of the sails by slowing up the air nearest to it and thereby causing the windstream to " somersault " and create eddies. Anyone who has hung over the rail of a big ship when under way (either from interest or necessity!) and gazed at the water alongside as the vessel passes through it, will have noticed that the water in immediate proximity to the side of the hull is pulled along at the same speed as that of the ship—owing to the surface friction of the hull

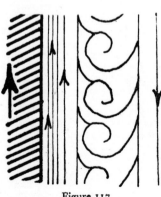

acting upon it—whereas a matter of a few feet or yards out from the hull (depending on the length and smoothness of the ship's skin) the water is not in horizontal motion. The outcome of this state of affairs is turbulence in the area between the static and moving water. Figure 117 will perhaps be of assistance in understanding this situation and the meaning of my use of the term " somersaulting eddies " ; the latter are in fact caused by forces similar to those

Figure 117

which tend to tip over the handlebars someone who, when bicycling along, applies the front brake too violently—the friction of the tyres on the road calls a halt, whilst the momentum of the unfortunate rider is too great to be stopped and so he leaves his perch unwillingly. It does not demand much imagination to realise that this is what does happen in practice as the windstream passes over the sails ; a little further thought will bring the realisation that the effect that this has on the efficiency of the sails is very serious, in that it breaks up the smooth flow of air which is so important.

It may perhaps be that if dinghy sailors spent a little more time smoothing down the whiskers on their sails and endeavouring to reduce the wind-mincing properties of bits and pieces of gadgetry festooning their masts, instead of quite so assiduously polishing the bottom of their boats, the resulting gains in speed would be more worth while. It is hard to know.

All this is quite interesting but the point is, if the foregoing remarks are acceptable, what can be done about it ? The idea of singeing the little projecting fibres of a sail is not one which will greatly appeal to those who cherish their sails very dearly, whilst treating them with some form of varnish or dope is also a method which will be viewed with diffidence. Smoothing down with a moderately warm iron will, however, be of at least temporary benefit, whilst brushing with a soft clothes-brush or wiping over with a damp cloth are also fairly effective ways of smoothing down the offending fibres. The strokes of the iron, brush or cloth should be parallel to the cloths or seams of sail—i.e., at about right-angles to the leech. This is approximately in the direction of the windflow over the sails.

* * * * *

Any major repairs to sails are best done by a sailmaker who knows what allowances to make for stretch when putting in large patches or pieces of fabric or roping. There are, nevertheless, many jobs which can easily be done by the amateur.

After the washing or rinsing process has been completed, the sails should be gone over, Sherlock Holmes fashion—" with a fine-toothed comb "—to seek out any weak seams, tears, unwhipped batten cords or chafed canvas. Seams which have come unstitched can usually be safely stitched up again with an ordinary sewing machine, but care must be taken to see that the tension on the thread is correct and not too taut, or puckering of the fabric will result. The most vulnerable places on the sails for broken stitching are the leech of the foresail and the cloths of the foresail at the leech end, especially where the sail is liable to get caught or rub on the diamond shroud spreaders. The mainsail pressing against the shrouds is apt to wear through the stitching. The inner ends of the batten pockets is another common place to find unstitched seams.

Chafe of the sails themselves is likely to occur where they are in contact with any fairly rigid object. Overlapping foresails are liable to chafe on the mainshrouds and crosstrees, while mainsails may also be worn by the same gear. Perhaps the most common

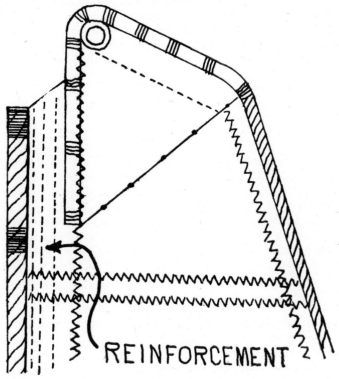

Figure 118

place for mainsails to chafe through is the luff near the headboard, between it and the bolt rope ; the sail is usually well reinforced at this place, as in Figure 118, but if the wear is excessive, the reinforcement should be increased. Battens which are too long will certainly wear a hole in the inboard end of their pockets, or through the sail itself ; but of course such battens should never be used, not only because of this fact, but because the sail cannot set well under such circumstances.

Very small holes torn in the sail can generally be sewn up with a needle and thread, using the herring-bone stitch, but larger tears or small holes which are caused by chafe should be patched. The reason for patching even small chafed holes is that the chafing is likely to have worn and weakened the fabric around the hole.

The herring-bone stitch is far more simple than a wordy explanation of it can be. Figure 119 will help to show what is done. The thread is first knotted and the needle pushed up through the cloth on the left-hand side of the tear ; see Figure 119a. It is then

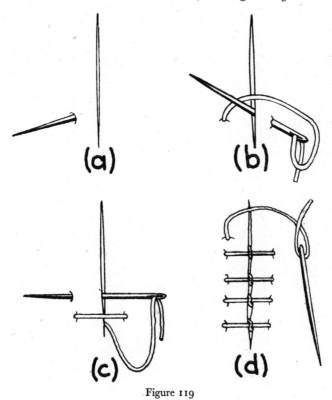

Figure 119

brought across to the other side of the tear and pushed down through the cloth opposite to the tear and at the same distance from the tear as the first insertion. The point of the needle is brought up between the fabric on either side of the tear and below the thread of the first part of the stitch. This stage is shown at (b) in Figure 119. The needle is then moved up a little for the next stitch and pushed up through the cloth on the left-hand side of the tear as described before ; this is the first stage of the second stitch and completes the first one (119c). This process is continued until the tear is made good. Figure 119d shows the finished stitches.

Patches are correctly made by interlocking the fabric of the patch with that around the hole to be repaired. The weak or thin fabric around the hole is cut away so that a square or triangular hole is left. A nick about ⅜-in. long is cut into each corner, as in Figure 120, and the edges folded back on themselves as shown in Figure 121. The patch is then prepared and should be ½-in. larger all round than the hole now bounded by the folded edges of the sail fabric. The edges of the patch are now folded inwards so as to make a flap of about ⅜-in.; Figure 122 shows this done, one side of the patch having been cut out of the drawing to show the other two folded edges more clearly. It should now be fairly easy to see how the edges of the canvas around the hole and the patch are interlocked, the patch edges being beneath the edges of the hole, as in the

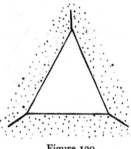

Figure 120

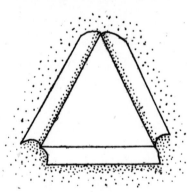

Figure 121

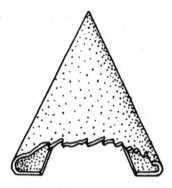

Figure 122

sectional sketch in Figure 123. The patch is now tacked in position and then sewn by machine. It will be found helpful if the folds which are made, are put in with the aid of a moderately warm iron and the patch pressed into position before the stitching commences.

The whipping at the ends of reef points, batten securing cords, and sometimes bolt ropes, occasionally comes adrift and the cord is then quickly unravelled. They should be re-whipped as soon as this is noticed. A palm and needle whipping is the one to use and is explained in Chapter III, page 41. Nylon cord can be secured from unravelling by holding the end in a flame for a few moments.

Figure 123

Some dinghy owners like to point the ends of the cords for retaining the battens in their pockets. This pointing makes the cords rather easier to push through the small holes in the ends of the battens themselves. The cords are really too small to be pointed in the normal manner adopted for ropes' ends because the cotton, of which they are usually made, is difficult stuff to handle and fluffs out in an awkward manner. The easiest way to do this pointing is to put on a whipping as described on page 36, but leaving about half an inch of cord beyond the whipping. This end is then unravelled, scraped and shaved down with a knife into a point. The tapered end is now twisted up and dipped in aircraft clear dope or synthetic resin glue. Varnish can be used, but is comparatively slow-drying and is liable to remain tacky a long time. One word of warning should be given in relation to synthetic resin glues used for this purpose ; some of these are in the form of a syrup to which must be added a hardener before it will set ; the hardener is an acid and will destroy fabric or cordage if it is allowed to come into direct contact with it, so great care must be taken to mix the acid thoroughly into the syrup before using it for the purpose of fixing a pointed cord end. If the foregoing precautions are taken no ill-effects should be suffered by the cord in proximity to the glue, but should the worst happen and the glue you are using have a decomposing effect on the cord, the whipping will, in any case, save the situation.

The easy sliding of the mainsail in the bolt rope groove of the mast may be facilitated by rubbing a candle up and down the rope in order to deposit a little wax upon it. This will both help to protect the inside of the groove from the weather and will much reduce the friction between the bolt rope and the wood.

If foresails are carefully looked after, no trouble should be experienced from the wire luff rope, but if the sails have been allowed to get saturated with salt and to remain in that condition, the wire rope may have rusted. In the case of white foresails, a rusty luff-rope will be indicated by red rust marks on the canvas around the rope, but with brown sails this sign may not be apparent. In the latter instance the luff should be held close to the ear and bent carefully backwards and forwards, whereupon a harsh grating noise will be heard if the wire is affected, or broken strands or wires may be heard clicking against one another; the ends of broken wires may even poke through the canvas and in this case it would most certainly be unwise to carry out the ritual washing dance described earlier in this chapter ! The cure for a rusty luff-rope lies with the sailmaker, who will renew it and the tabling surrounding it and securing it to the sail.

Spinnakers have hardly been mentioned in these two chapters on sails, but they are perhaps more tolerant of casual treatment than the other sails on a dinghy. Apart from the washing or rinsing of cotton spinnakers, all that they usually require is fairly frequent attention with needle and thread to the little holes and tears to which they are rather susceptible. Although nylon spinnakers will not rot to any extent, they should be kept as dry as possible, so that they will be light and set easily in faint airs ; salt should therefore be rinsed from them, for it attracts moisture from the air and so will be liable to add to the weight of the sail.

If a sail gets affected by mildew, which produces black spots on the fabric, every effort must be made to kill the fungus and entirely eliminate it from the sail. The best way to do this is to get it 100 per cent dry and free from salt. It should then be laid flat and brushed with a stiff clothes-brush, after which it should be hung up and beaten (not near any other sails) so that all the fungi and their spores are shaken out of the fabric. Finally it can be scrubbed with a hot, weak solution of washing soda and very thoroughly rinsed and carefully dried. There are several brands of rot-proofing liquids on the market, some of which give quite satisfactory results.

The process of colouring, waterproofing and anti-mildewing sails, popular in larger classes of boat, has been treated with caution by the dinghy-racing fraternity. There is one reason, other than purely aesthetic, for colouring sails ; a well chosen colour may be more restful to the eyes on sunny days than is a glaring white sail. However, I do not think that it is quite so easy to see what the wind is doing in a coloured sail, and, since the luff of the foresail is the part of one's sail to be watched when going to windward, I prefer a white foresail, though for many years I used a mainsail made from brown cloth, which was very easy on the eyes. Since the sail was made from a coloured cloth and not dyed after being sewn up, I have no experience which would enable me to say whether or not dyeing alters the shape. Anti-mildew treatment is well worth while and waterproofing is particularly valuable ; neither of these processes affect the shape of the sail and they only add a fraction to the weight—which is saved many times over if the sails are being rained upon or spray soaked.

INDEX